CHEESE
BEER WINE CIDER

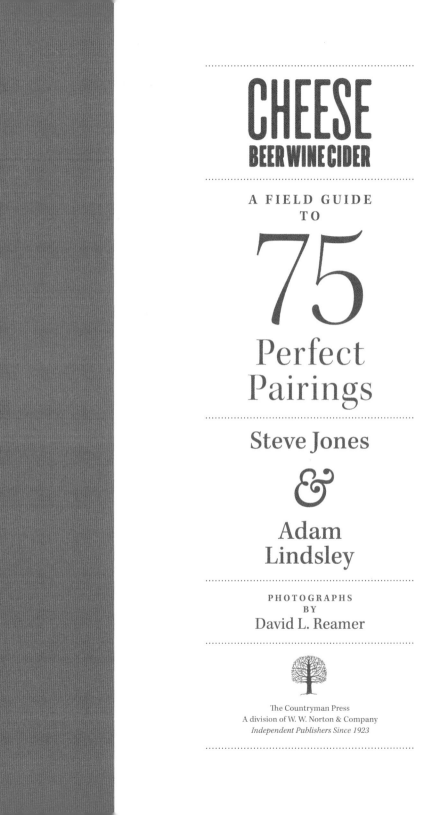

CHEESE
BEER WINE CIDER

A FIELD GUIDE
TO

75

Perfect
Pairings

Steve Jones

&

Adam
Lindsley

PHOTOGRAPHS
BY
David L. Reamer

The Countryman Press
A division of W. W. Norton & Company
Independent Publishers Since 1923

CONTENTS

STEVE JONES:
HOW I GOT INTO CHEESE

"**W**ine and cheese are ageless companions, like aspirin and aches, or June and moon, or good people and noble ventures."

So said *The Gastronomical Me* and *The Art of Eating* author M. F. K. Fisher, and she knew a thing or two about food. Who can counter an argument framed with such eloquence?

Convention dictates that when you slice into a creamy Brie, a funky Camembert, or a nutty Gruyère, prying the cork from a vintage Bordeaux or crisp Beaujolais Blanc is the logical next step. The concept that wine is *the* beverage to pair with cheese is so ingrained in the public mind-set that diners pay it allegiance without sparing a single thought on the actual experience.

At Cheese Bar and Chizu, my shops in Portland, Oregon, I serve wine with the 250 varieties of cheese lovingly crammed in the display case. I also serve beer and cider, both on tap and in bottles. It makes sense to have all three on hand, because each beverage is a worthy suitor for the right cheese.

But what *is* the right cheese? Most people go in blind, their dutiful faith in the "wine and cheese" conceit setting them up for a game of culinary Russian roulette in which the loser receives a menagerie of off-putting flavors spread like butter over the palate. One of the great joys of my dual job as a cheesemonger and bar owner is steering my customers in the right direction, offering tried-and-true recommendations that I picked up the only way I knew how: firsthand experiences.

Those experiences began in the mid-nineties, when I had the fortuitous and life-changing opportunity to work in a fantastic wine shop in St. Louis called the Wine Merchant. Every day, we sold magnificent vintages from the premier winemaking regions of the world. Then, the challenge was given to me to create and curate a cheese counter that focused not only on the classic cheeses of Europe, but also the wonderful American artisan and farmstead cheeses that were experiencing a simultaneous rebirth and awakening. So, alongside the imported Parmigiano-

Reggiano, Manchego, and Comté, we had cheeses from Vermont Shepherd, Juniper Grove, and Roth Kase. Every evening, we drank Puligny-Montrachet or Champagne, and then we finished the night sampling the American craft beers that were coming to light for the first time for us.

Of course, to fuel our explorations we depended on a quantity of the great cheese we were selling every day. While enjoying these cheeses and beverages together, I initially stumbled across some immaculate pairings. As I continued, I started to lean on what I had learned until I had accumulated a portfolio of good matches and solid rules to use for pairing cheese not only with wine, but with beer. Everyone knew, it seemed, that cheese went well with wine, but we were finding it went just as well, if not even better, with beer. Then, one night, someone showed up with a cider from the Normandy region of France, and I was immediately convinced that the beverage also had fantastic merit with cheese.

As we and our customers continued to enjoy cheese with wine, beer, and cider, I discovered that each balanced notable merits with flaws. For example, wine often carries a lovely acidity that works well with cheese, but its tannins can discolor flavors. Beer has an effervescence that scrubs the palate clean, keeping it sharp and lively, but hops can crush subtle notes in younger cheeses. Cider associates quite nicely with many cheeses, but the beverage has not yet matched the stylistic breadth of beer and wine (though it's certainly well on its way). Through the years, I have presented cheese with many different beverages: coffee, tea, Scotch, vodka, even a few colas. But beer, wine, and cider are the three that most interest people.

In 2012, the organizers of *Bon Appétit*'s first annual Feast Portland event invited me to moderate a panel on the virtues of wine and beer with cheese. Teaming up with Joshua Wesson (cofounder of the Best Cellars wine shops in New York) and Christian DeBenedetti (author

ONE GOOD PAIRING WAS ALL IT TOOK TO OPEN THEIR EYES TO POSSIBILITIES THEY MIGHT NEVER HAVE IMAGINED

of *The Great American Ale Trail*), we agreed to steer our presentation away from the format of a stodgy lecture (where it quite easily could have gone) and toward the looser, more approachable concept of a SMACKDOWN!

Riffing off a boxing theme, I played referee to Wesson's and DeBenedetti's five rounds of wine vs. beer bouts, and the results were not only hilarious but educational. The crowd ate it up, and the event's success led to other "smackdowns" with such participants as James Beard Award–winning writer and wine connoisseur David Lynch. I began to make it a point to convince wine aficionados like Lynch to try cheese with something other than their favorite bottles of red or white. It was just a matter of tearing down the mental walls that have kept cheese lovers from exploring a stunning new world of flavors. The amazing thing to me was how often and how quickly I could take people from the "wine and cheese is always best" camp and flip them to the beer and cider camp. Usually one good pairing was all it took to open their eyes to possibilities they might never have imagined without that first push.

Let me share one other story with you that had a profound impact on my way of thinking. A number of years ago, while journeying through France's Savoie region en route to Piedmont, I somehow convinced my fellow travelers to stop and take a short hike up one of the absolutely gorgeous mountains we were passing through. We pulled off the motorway and found a sign that read simply "Source of the Glacier," situated at the base of a rough trail leading up the mountainside. Off we went. About a kilometer up the trail, we encountered a small hut, not much to look at, just a simple little hut that had obviously been there quite some time. But upon closer inspection, we discovered it was actually a bar serving local cheese, simple food, and beers from the region! As hungry and thirsty as we were by that point, we weren't certain whether it was real or whether we had stepped off the trail and into the afterlife. Everything tasted ten times better than it would have in any other setting, and it cemented my resolve that beer and cheese would not go uncelebrated on my watch. I will never forget that moment!

And thus the idea for this book was born. At Cheese Bar and Chizu here in Portland, I find myself offering advice on which beverages to pair with cheese six days a week. I've been commissioned year after year to provide cheese pairings for beer and cider events, and it's both challenging and rewarding. I've developed a knack for it, I'm not too humble to say, but there's always something new to learn and a new combination to explore. It's that sense of experimentation that runs through the heart of this book, and the quality I most want you, the reader, to take from it.

More than anything, sampling cheeses with these brilliant drinks should be Fun with a capital *F*. If this book is even half as fun to read as it was to write, we're in good shape.

–STEVE

PREPARING TO EAT CHEESE WITH BEER, WINE, AND CIDER, A.K.A "IT'S ALL IN THE DETAILS"

Take a good look at that lovely hunk of Roquefort up there. Admire its undulating surface, its potent blue-green network of pockets and tendrils infiltrating a fudgelike body and releasing a bold, tangy burst of flavor the instant it hits your tongue. You can practically taste it, can't you? It's perfection. Perfection embodied by aged and mold-inoculated sheep's milk.

But that intensely flavorful, complex, gorgeous cheese didn't spring into existence through a random function of nature. You won't find wedges of the stuff growing wild in undisturbed grottos or on damp forest floors next to the chanterelles. Someone (and very likely, several someones) guided the milk from udder to curd to wheel, closely following a time-honored, painstaking process over a span of months and even years to get that beautiful blue on your plate.

Likewise, properly pairing cheese with beer, wine, or cider is no accident. If you're new to the world of purchasing, storing, and serving cheese and alcohol, then it's frightfully easy for a tasting session to go south. Myriad considerations need to be made, from the temperature at which you serve your cheese to the best place to store beverages.

Conversely, the more experienced reader may not need a single word of this chapter and can skip straight to the recommended pairings in Part II. That's okay; this particular chunk of the book is not for them.

It's for you, whether you're a long-time wine fanatic looking to expand into the realm of cheese, a die-hard cheese enthusiast seeking a primer on beer and cider, or completely new to all of it. The information that follows will put you on a level playing field with the veteran cheese eater and the seasoned epicurean. Putting in the work now to learn this stuff will pay off big time in the form of a fun and stress-free tasting session. You don't *need* to follow the guidelines we're about to lay out, but doing so will heighten the experience for you and anyone you bring along for the ride.

THE 9 RULES OF BUYING, STORING, AND SERVING CHEESE

RULE #1
BUY WHAT YOU CAN USE IN A WEEK.

A visit to your local cheese shop is by turns a feast for the senses and a test of willpower. Standing before the glass, it's easy to go overboard with all those lovely white and yellow and blue-veined wheels singing their siren's song, convincing you that buying a wedge of at least half them is not only a good idea, but perhaps the best idea you've had all month. Why not load up while you have the chance?

DON'T DO THIS Here's why it's a bad idea to buy that much cheese at once: Chances are, you don't have a cave at home. And you don't have the climate-controlled display cases all the best cheesemongers use. What do you have? The refrigerator. And the refrigerator simply isn't an optimal environment for prolonging a cheese's life span. Fridges sap moisture from cheese and bombard it with foul smells and flavors from whatever else you've got socked away in there.

Another reason not to horde your cheese for weeks on end: cheesemongers aren't sitting on a cache of cheese they've been stockpiling for years, waiting for you to come along and buy it (or at least, they shouldn't be). They're selling it at its peak, when it's meant to be eaten. Sure, if it gets moldy, you can just cut it away and eat what remains, but good cheese isn't cheap, so why risk wasting any of it?

Instead, be smart and just buy what you can consume in a week's time. If you're using this book to set up a tasting session, then don't buy more than five different cheeses at a time. You should stick to under a quarter-pound of total cheese per person, but feel free to use the following chart to determine how many ounces of each cheese to buy for your guests. Your cheese will look better, smell better, and taste better when you don't give the refrigerator a chance to wipe its greasy little fingers all over it. Because it will, and there's little you can do to stop it.

ounces of cheese to buy

Number of Cheeses	Number of People				
	THREE	SIX	TEN	FIFTEEN	TWENTY
ONE	12	24	40	60	80
TWO	6	12	20	30	40
THREE	4	8	13	20	27
FOUR	3	6	10	15	20
FIVE	2	5	8	12	16
SIX	2	4	7	10	13
SEVEN	2	3	6	9	11
EIGHT	2	3	5	8	10

RULE #2
KEEP CHEESE OUT OF THE FREEZER.

Some people feel justified in breaking Rule #1 by doing to cheese what they do with anything else perishable they buy in bulk: tossing it into the freezer.

DON'T DO THIS When you freeze cheese, you're proudly announcing to the world, "I don't deserve nice things." Your freezer is cheese's archnemesis, a mortal enemy with the power to introduce ice crystals that destroy the delicate textures the cheesemaker worked so hard to create.

Your cheese deserves better than that. You deserve better than that. Don't freeze the cheese. Make it your mantra.

RULE #3
SERVE CHEESE AT ROOM TEMPERATURE.

Okay, you bought your cheese, you got it home without smashing it under the rest of your groceries, it's been chilling out in the ol' Frigidaire, and the day of the tasting has arrived. The single biggest rookie move you can make here—and we've all done it at one time or another—is to serve the cheese straight out of the fridge.

For goodness' sake, *don't do this.*

Cold cheese pales in comparison to what you could be eating if you just let it come to room temperature before digging into it. Half an hour out of the fridge for fresh cheeses, such as chèvre, and 45 minutes to an hour for everything else is what you should be shooting for. The cheese's natural aromas, flavors, and textures will reach their peak, making for a much more enjoyable experience for everyone involved.

Don't let it sit out for too long, though. After a couple of hours out of the refrigerator have passed, cheese will start to "weep," losing liquid as it oxidizes and hardens. Unless you like your cheese the consistency of day-old flank steak, you'll want to eat it in that peak zone between the time it reaches room temperature and about an hour after that.

RULE #4
SERVE CHEESE ON WOOD.

If you're serious about cheese, and you're serious about presentation, then arranging your cheeses on a dinner plate is not going to cut it. Wood—particularly dark wood—is the best option for serving cheese for one very, very important reason:

It looks good.

Aesthetics play a substantial role in the joys of a cheese tasting, and wood makes for a beautiful vehicle upon which to display your selection. Remember, cheese is a living thing. Presenting it on something else that's living (or at least something that used to be) helps it, well, come alive.

Don't have a fancy wood block or even a wooden cutting board? You can make one fairly easily with a small plank of leftover wood from the hardware store, some sandpaper, and some mineral oil.

If you absolutely do not have anything flat and wooden in the house besides the tabletop itself, then a slab of slate or terra-cotta will do in a pinch. But you may have a harder time tracking either of those down than a cheap $10 board from Target.

RULE #5
DON'T PRECUT THE CHEESE.

Say you have three guests at your cheese tasting in addition to yourself. Your natural instinct is probably to slice each of the cheeses into four equal pieces. You know, as a courtesy.

Some courtesy! Cheese dries up quickly and loses flavor when exposed to oxygen. Opening up new surface areas on the cheese just accelerates this process.

Instead, leave the wedge or block intact (with the rind!) and let your guests carve off what they want as they go. People will undoubtedly favor one cheese over another, so letting their tastes determine how much of each to eat is just good etiquette. When they dig in, instruct them to take a little at a time and to slice from center to rind (see image).

RULE #6
DON'T WORRY ABOUT FANCY KNIVES.

Yeah, $600 razor-sharp 3-inch carbon steel blades with handles carved from mother-of-pearl by Tibetan monks are pretty and all, but why blow that cash on something a butter knife can do nearly as well? If you're spending money on classing up your tasting sessions, then follow Rule #4 and invest in some lovely wood serving blocks instead. Or more cheese!

Do butter knives really work? Yes, but your steak knives work even better. Anything that can shear away a small sample without crushing the wedge in the process will do. Don't worry about cross-contamination between the cheeses: one knife per person is just fine.

And cheese planes? Gouging, mutilating, abusive cheese planes? Don't get me *started* on cheese planes.

RULE #7
ARRANGE CHEESE BY DEPTH OF FLAVOR.

When deciding how to present your cheese (on a wood block, I hope?), taste a small slice of each one first. Which has the lightest flavor? Which has the strongest? You'll want to arrange your selection from mildest to boldest. So, that lovely fresh burrata and that superstinky Époisses should be on opposite ends of your board, with everything else in between.

Also, take the shape of the cheese into consideration during placement. If you start with a wedge, place a rectangular cheese next to it, and maybe a nice molded round one next to that. The contrast is striking and appealing. It's also worth varying the color of the cheeses. Remember, "The eye eats first."

RULE #8
KEEP THE ACCOMPANIMENTS SIMPLE.

A face-melting Eddie Van Halen guitar solo is a wonderful thing. So are the mellow tones of the French horn solo in Tchaikovsky's Fifth Symphony. But combine them and you've got a dissonant mess that does neither any favors.

The same care should be taken when deciding what, if anything, you're going to serve at your cheese tasting. The cheese and the beverages you're serving it with should be the stars of the show, so really you're just looking for a palate cleanser between the cheese-and-alcohol combinations. Here are some good things to serve on the side at your next tasting session:

- Glass of water
- Plain crackers
- Bread
- Nuts
- Mild fruit, such as apples or pears

Avoid:

- Flavored crackers
- Anything spicy
- Pickled items
- Honey (see the Quick Bite for more details)

QUICK BITE

Serving Honey with Cheese

Order cheese at a restaurant and invariably you'll find a smear of honey on the plate, or even drizzled directly over the cheese. This is perfectly acceptable if the chef has tasted the honey and the cheese beforehand and knows they pair well together. The problem with blindly recommending honey as an accoutrement is that honey has such a vast range of flavors, from cotton-candy sweet all the way to medicinal and bitter, based on the nectar of the flower or flowers from which it was made. Try a clover and a buckwheat honey side by side and the difference is immediately apparent. Rather than recommend something that may or may not complement your cheese and beverages, it's best to avoid honey altogether in your at-home tasting sessions.

RULE #9
STORE LEFTOVERS IN AN AIRTIGHT CONTAINER.

The tasting's over, and somehow, you and your fellow turophiles (cheese dorks) managed to show a little restraint and leave some nibbles behind. Just wrap 'em in plastic wrap and toss 'em back in the fridge, right?

No. Not right.

Reducing exposure to the air is important in helping cheese retain its integrity, but equally important is letting the cheese breathe. That's why your cheesemonger wrapped it in that special cheese paper and why you should do everything in your power to replicate those conditions. If you've lost or thrown away the cheese paper, wrapping the cheese in parchment or wax paper and then sealing it in a resealable plastic bag or plastic tub will prolong its life well past the life span suggested in Rule #1.

ALL ABOUT ALCOHOL

By now it should be obvious where I stand on the merits of cheese; that I've made it my life's work should be evidence enough. But adding beer, wine, or cider to the equation can complement cheese in ways that make seeking out a good match a major treat for the senses.

Toying with cheese-and-beverage pairings opens up near-infinite combinations and rewards experimentation. Even when you come upon a complete and miserable failure (and you will), those mistakes provide valuable lessons, even more so than the successes. With so many new breweries, wineries, and cideries popping up every month, the next great matchup is one trip to the bottle shop away.

As I mentioned at the start of this book, my whole outlook on pairing cheese with alcohol made enormous strides in the mid-nineties during my tenure at the Wine Merchant in St. Louis. Curating the shop's cheese counter while drinking our fine wines and the craft beers from local breweries, such as Schlafly, gave me an affinity for quality beverages that brought the cheeses I sold to life. My palate gradually developed and I started to appreciate the nuances in what I was consuming, learning the difference between a good drink and a great one.

The experience taught me, among many other things, to buy my alcohol from a reputable source that does good business and turns a lot of product over. Doing so almost invariably nets you fresher beverages that just taste better than those that have been sitting on a shelf since the Reagan administration.

Entire tomes can be and have been written on the minutia of "proper" alcohol handling. We don't have that kind of time and this isn't that kind of book, so we're going to get straight to the important stuff, the Need to Knows of the holy trinity of beer, wine, and cider.

STORAGE

BEER Ever had a European lager from its iconic green bottle? If so, you have almost certainly experienced the unpleasant skunky aromas and flavors that result when hop compounds become exposed to light.

Brown bottles do a decent job of keeping the light out, but green bottles fail spectacularly at it. It's why so many Americans actually think that's what European beer—which often makes its transatlantic journey in green bottles—is supposed to taste like. Try those same beers from their home breweries, or even from a can, and you'll see what you've been missing.

Skunked beer is an abomination, an assault on the senses, and the best way you can combat it (besides not buying beer in green bottles) is by keeping your beer in a cool, dark place. In other words, your refrigerator. Store bottles upright to allow the yeast to settle to the bottom, and toward the back of the fridge to avoid temperature fluctuations.

Also, beer is best consumed fresh. Some bigger beers, such as barleywines and imperial stouts, can withstand years of cellaring and develop intriguing new flavors in the process. They're the exception, not the rule. Check the bottling date on your beer and only buy what you plan on drinking within a couple months of it.

WINE Unlike beer, wine does not go all skunky when bathed in direct light. However, that doesn't mean you should leave that $40 bottle of cab franc sitting on your kitchen windowsill until you're ready to pop the cork. Heat is the single most destructive force against wine, and forcing it to endure a hot, enclosed area will only accelerate the aging process and produce undesirable flavors. Again, dark and cool is the name of the game.

For those without a cellar that maintains a fairly stable temperature, a wine cooler is an easy solution, if you're willing to throw down a little extra money. A good wine cooler will allow you to store your wine in the ideal range of 50 to 55 degrees Fahrenheit. They go from about $100 for the smallest models to several thousand dollars for the largest, top-of-the-line options.

Most people who aren't storing wine long-term shouldn't worry too much about their wine going bad and just store it in a pantry, cupboard, or basement. Some wine aficionados will insist on storing them sideways to help the lees settle and keep the cork from drying out, but again, if you're not planning on keeping that wine for years, don't worry about it.

CIDER While people have very strong opinions about how to store beer and wine (so much so that we're positive *someone* out there disagrees with our previous suggestions), not much has been said about how best to keep your cider in prime condition.

Our thoughts on the matter are simple: The cool, dark environment of your refrigerator offers the same protection against off-flavors as it does your beer, so why overthink it? For those with a wine cellar, feel free to store your cider alongside your prized vintages; for the rest of us, just stick with the fridge.

SERVING BEER, WINE, AND CIDER

The day of the tasting has come. You've done your homework and bought fresh beer, good wine, and quality cider. Why go to all the trouble of *acquiring* these wonderful tipples without going the extra mile and *serving* them properly?

You may be thinking, *What's with all these rules? Shouldn't drinking be fun?* Yes, it should! But you wouldn't drink an ice-cold red wine from a Dixie cup, would you? Or a room-temperature pilsner from a punch bowl? It pays to have a little know-how about how you're serving your intoxicating libations. What follows is by no means scripture, more a road map to fermented bliss by the glass.

SERVING TEMPERATURES

BEER Just as you shouldn't eat your cheese straight from the refrigerator, most (but not all) beers taste better a little closer to room temperature. Typically, the lighter stuff is best served cold, whereas the darker, heavier beers see their flavors bloom at warmer levels. See the following list for the suggested lengths of time to pull various types of beer from your fridge before your tasting session.

STRAIGHT OUT OF THE FRIDGE

- Pilsner
- Helles
- Kölsch
- Hefeweizen

15 MINUTES OUT OF THE FRIDGE

- Pale ale
- IPA
- Amber/red/brown ale
- Dubbel

- Sour ale
- Most Belgian ales (golden ale, Belgian IPA, wit)
- Saison
- Bock/doppelbock

30 MINUTES OUT OF THE FRIDGE

- British ales (ESB, mild)
- Porter
- Stout
- Barleywine
- Tripel
- Quad

WINE   With red wine, the general rule of thumb is that it's best served at or just below room temperature (if your room is in the 60 to 70 degrees Fahrenheit range, anyway), but that isn't always the case. For example, I like my pinot noir slightly cool, somewhere in the upper 50s/low 60s. So, I'll put the bottle in the fridge for 20 to 30 minutes before serving. Same goes for light reds, such as gamay or Lambrusco.

White wines are another matter—they're almost always better when chilled. The following times indicate when to pull chilled bottles out of the fridge *before* you start drinking them.

STRAIGHT OUT OF THE FRIDGE [SPARKLING AND LIGHT-BODIED WHITE WINES]

- Champagne
- Sauvignon blanc
- Riesling/other German and Alsatian varietals
- Pinot grigio
- Rosé
- Moscato

20 MINUTES OUT OF THE FRIDGE [MEDIUM- AND FULL-BODIED WHITE WINES]

- Chardonnay
- Viognier
- Beaujolais
- Marsanne
- Sémillon
- Verdicchio
- Grüner Veltliner

CIDER When deciding how warm or cold your cider should be, consider whether there are flavors in the cider you want to accentuate or flavors you want to subdue.

For instance, dry ciders with funky wild yeast do better between 50 and 55 degrees Fahrenheit, because it encourages more of their distinct characteristics to surface. These types of ciders do well in a cellar environment (again, if you have one).

On the other end of the spectrum, to tone down sweeter, fruit-driven ciders (which make up most of the current cider market), serve them straight from the refrigerator.

GLASSWARE

It's so easy to get sucked into the wide world of glasses. Glassware manufacturers insist that drinking every beverage from its proper glass significantly improves its aroma and flavor. And to a certain extent, having the proper glass can enhance the experience of a particular drink. A tall, thin-walled weizen glass is the ideal show-case for your fluffy-headed wheat beers, and chardonnays just seem to shine in a wineglass with a large bowl. Ciders have all manner of interesting region-specific receptacles, from wooden cups to hollowed-out ram's horns.

However, it is our opinion that most of what a stemware manufacturer promises its glasses can accomplish is simply marketing. Can you really detect a veritable fruit stand of new flavors if you're drinking that Malbec from a pinot noir glass instead of the glass "specially designed" for Malbec? Please.

You don't need to invest in Riedel's entire catalog to enjoy every variety of wine to their fullest, and the same goes for beer and cider. If you use just one type of glass for your cheese-and-beverage tastings, make it an ordinary wineglass or tulip-shaped glass. Both channel aromas up and out of the vessel and work beautifully for beer, wine, or cider. Riedel's entry-level Ouverture series is a fine, less wallet-emptying place to start. Feel free to expand your collection from there, but spending that money on more cheese, beer, wine, and cider is a better course of action.

Whatever temporary housing you choose for your beverages, it's crucial to level the playing field. I've seen beer-and-wine tasting competitions where the wine was poured into immaculately polished stemware while the beer was served in plastic cups. No joke! Treat your beverages with equal respect to get the most out of all of them.

POURING

BEER When pouring a beer, follow these simple steps for maximum enjoyment:

1. Rinse out the glass to remove any lingering particles of soap or dust.

2. Tilt your glass at a 45-degree angle and pour down the side of the glass to avoid churning up too much foam.

3. Depending on how many people are present for your tasting, you might not get to pour more than a few ounces of the beer before moving on to the next glass. But if you're tasting solo, keep pouring down the side of the glass until it's about two-thirds full, then tilt the glass upright and pour straight into the center of the liquid to form a lovely head to your beer that's about an inch thick. A proper head amplifies the flavor of the beer by allowing the hop, yeast, and malt aromas to blossom, preparing your palate for what's to come.

It's also best not to pour your beer too far in advance. That way you'll keep it from getting too oxidized. Not a huge chance of that happening, but why take it at all?

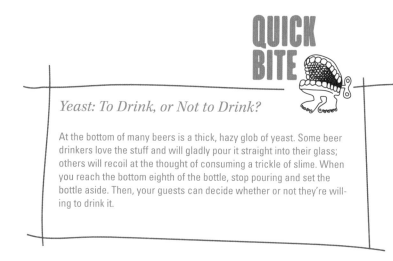

QUICK BITE

Yeast: To Drink, or Not to Drink?

At the bottom of many beers is a thick, hazy glob of yeast. Some beer drinkers love the stuff and will gladly pour it straight into their glass; others will recoil at the thought of consuming a trickle of slime. When you reach the bottom eighth of the bottle, stop pouring and set the bottle aside. Then, your guests can decide whether or not they're willing to drink it.

WINE You don't need to be a sommelier to pour wine well, but it helps to know a little trick to keep from dribbling the wine on your table (or your guests!). Pour the wine straight into the center of an upright glass, and when you're ready to stop, twist the edge of the bottle closest to the floor away from you as you tilt the bottle up.

As you near the bottom of the bottle, you'll want to be careful not to pour out the gritty, unpleasant sediment. At the first sign of dregs in your pour, stop immediately!

QUICK BITE

Decanting

Chances are you've heard about letting red wine "breathe" by decanting it from the bottle into another vessel and leaving it to sit for an hour or two. Certain wine aficionados swear by this time-honored practice, whereas others declare it nothing more than a myth and a waste of your time. If you're not already in one camp or the other, it's worth trying it out with two identical bottles of wine. Just open one bottle and let it breathe for two hours in a larger receptacle, then open the other bottle when you're ready to compare the two. If you're convinced letting the wine breathe was a good idea, then stick with it. If not, stop worrying about it.

CIDER Although a frothy head is desirable with beer, that's not the case with cider. Carbonated cider can be a delicate thing, so pouring it as smoothly as possible down the inside of a tilted glass helps retain its effervescence. This is less of an issue with still (noncarbonated) cider, but a steady hand remains our method of choice.

Alternatively, you can perform quite a spectacle and pour your cider the Spanish way by putting as much distance between bottle and glass as possible. It's entertaining as hell, but it's Foam City if you try it with a sparkling cider. Read more about it on page 181.

TASTING TIPS

After arranging the cheeses on whatever surface you're serving them on (surely by now, you know where I stand on that), it's time to get down to the business of consuming all these earthly delights. Just a few more pointers and you're on your way.

PLACE SETTING Give every participant his or her own small plate (to hold inedible rinds, mostly) and knife. There will be a lot of finger-to-cheese contact, so don't forget the napkins.

ORDER It's not a bad idea to go lightest to strongest. Decide whether you're going to let the beverages dictate the order you taste, or the cheeses (if you're pairing multiple cheeses). Or you can just let your guests go in any order that pleases them. There's no wrong way to go about it, as long as everyone's having fun.

NOTE-TAKING Depending on how serious you want to take your session, provide your guests with pen and paper to jot down their own tasting notes, and wait until everyone's tried the same cheese-plus-beverage combination before talking about it. I recommend this approach because it's so easy to guide tasters' palates toward one flavor through the power of suggestion, making them think they tasted one thing when in fact they might have tasted something completely different before you said anything.

CHEWING AND TASTING Here's the best way I've found to combine the cheese and your selected beverage for the optimum pairing experience:

1. Slice off a small thumbnail-size chunk of cheese, then ball it up between your forefinger and thumb to get a feel for the texture and the oil content.
2. Pop the cheese in your mouth, but don't chew it just yet!
3. Press the cheese to the roof of your mouth with your tongue and then take a sip of the beverage.
4. Making sure it's immersed in the beverage, chew the cheese, trying to combine it with the beverage as much as possible before swallowing.
5. Wait at least 10 seconds to ensure you taste any lingering flavors on the finish.
6. Take a sip of water or bite of bread to cleanse your palate, then try another combo!

CUTTING THE TETHER: TIPS FOR MAKING NEW PAIRINGS, NO MATTER WHERE YOU ARE

Maybe you don't feel like following the recommended pairings we worked so tirelessly to document for you in the next section of the book. Maybe you've worked through every one and you're ready to branch out into unexplored territory.

Or maybe you're sitting at your favorite restaurant, your eyes glazing over as you stare at their beverage list, wondering which one will pair best with the three very different cheeses on that cheese plate you just ordered.

Either way, I say, "Bravo!"

I also say, "Wait! I have a few more tips to share with you! You're gonna want to hear these!"

THE 3 PILLARS OF MATCHMAKING

When searching for the perfect marriage between cheese and beer, wine, or cider, pick one of the following three guidelines to increase your chances of striking gold:

COMPARABLE Similar flavors have a knack for going well together. Some examples: a tangy fresh cow's milk cheese with a tart Spanish sidra, rich mascarpone with a sweet Moscato, or a smoky blue cheese with a roasty stout. Just be careful not to go overboard. For example, a very fruity cheese and a very fruity rosé may be inviting palate fatigue, so show a little restraint.

CONTRASTING Pairing a big, boozy, bourbon barrel–aged stout with a simple triple-crème may not sound like the most intuitive match, but opposites invite all manner of flavorful dovetailing. In this example, the beer and cheese create a sort of "coffee and cream" profile that's delightful to experience. Sweet and salty usually works well, too (e.g. a dessert wine, such as a Sauternes, with Roquefort).

REGIONAL "What grows together goes together." So goes the saying and so say we. Terroir—the unique combination of environmental conditions (soil, air, microorganisms) of a specific location—stamps an indelible mark on cheeses and beverages made in the same general area, creating a sort of throughline that invites complementary pairings. Think Camembert and a Norman cider.

BEWARE OF EXTREMES

I love supersour beers and nuclear-potent cheeses, but those bold, assertive flavors are very difficult to pair properly. Say you've got a big, stinky blue cheese that makes your tongue ache just thinking about it. You can crush it (say, with a massive 15% ABV barrel-aged barleywine), but good luck finding a balanced match.

PAIRING CHEESE IN RESTAURANTS

Although it's likely you'll do the vast majority of your cheese, beer, wine, and cider tasting at home, where you control what you serve and how you serve it, dining out forces you to work with much stricter guardrails. Don't be intimidated: It's loads

of fun, because you get to play detective and start asking the important questions: *What's this cheese going to taste like? What about that one? This menu has six wines by the glass, three beers on draft, and one (bottled) cider . . . which should I order?*

Just about any restaurant fancy enough to offer a cheese plate is going to serve alcohol as well; the challenge comes with finding a beverage that really clicks with at least one and preferable two or three cheeses on the plate. It depends entirely on what that particular restaurant's pouring on that particular day, so you're pretty much at the mercy of its menu.

You're not going in completely unarmed, though. I mean, you bought this book, so you're already three steps ahead of that handsome couple the next table over who decided to wing it and deeply regret choosing that flabby cabernet sauvignon to sip between bites of a fatty Brillat-Savarin. Here's how to turn someone else's cheese board into a memorable experience, starting with the most ideal solution:

OPTION 1 Bring this book with you!
Look at what cheeses are offered. Are any of them covered in this book? (Quickest way to check: skim each pairing chapter list on pages 39, 97, and 153, or the index on page 220.) If so, see if the restaurant serves any of the beers, wines, or ciders we paired with those cheeses. You may get lucky and hit the jackpot! If not, give Option 2 a shot . . .

OPTION 2 Play it safe, go with a cider.
Check the drinks menu for a cider. If the restaurant serves one, go with that. Cider pairs seamlessly with more cheeses than beer or wine combined, so it will always be a safe choice. No cider on the menu? Move down to Option 3 . . .

OPTION 3 Find a connection.
When you know which cheeses you'll be eating, look them up online if you're not sure what they taste like. *Culture Magazine*'s website offers wonderful summaries of most cheeses if you need a quick reference. Once you generally know what you're in for, go through the Comparable, Contrasting, and Regional list on page 34 and see whether you can use one of those criteria to make a match. If there's a stinky, funky cheese on the plate, is a wild ale available? Is there a semisweet cider you can drink with that supersalty pecorino? Manchego's a cheese plate staple; do they have rioja by the glass to complete this taste of Spain?

OPTION 4 Ask the waiter.
Waitstaff worth their salt will have at least an inkling of what the featured cheeses taste like, and they should also be able to provide a general description of the beers, wines, and ciders on their menu. If the restaurant employs a sommelier (or a cice-

rone, the even rarer beer equivalent of a house wine expert), that person likely will have some strong opinions about what to drink with the cheeses, so listen to what he or she has to say. In the absence of certified experts, it pays to exercise caution when it comes to a restaurant's recommended pairings printed on the menu (this goes for non-cheese dishes, too). These are pretty hit or miss, in our experience, with the beverage and cheese combinations seldom rising above inoffensively existing in the same space. A little education goes a long way, so only resort to the restaurant's default suggestions if you're totally lost on what to order.

ONE LAST PIECE OF ADVICE: DON'T BE AFRAID OF FAILURE

Hitting a bum pairing once in a while is as inevitable as dropped toast landing jelly-side down. Expect it to happen, but remember that these so-called failures are an important instructive experience. As I mentioned earlier, sometimes you can learn more about what does and doesn't work by the failures than the successes. It teaches you to ask, "Well, why *didn't* this turn out like I thought it would?" Soon you'll be savvy enough to instinctively home in on worthwhile pairings left and right. The sky's the limit, and there's a world of cheese, beer, wine, and cider out there just begging to be experimented with. Be fearless!

## Part II

THE PAIRINGS

CHEESE WITH
BEER

DEATH & TAXES 40
BEAR HILL 42
MIMOLETTE 44
CHESHIRE 47
FRESH CHÈVRE 49
TORTA DEL CASAR 52
LORELEI 55

BIG WOODS BLUE 57
BRIE 60
QUADRELLO DI BUFALA 62
TRIVIUM 65
NANCY'S CAMEMBERT 67
MAHON RESERVA 69
CHARLOE 71
NIMBLE 73
OFF KILTER 76
LANCASHIRE 78
AGED CHEDDAR 81
ÉPOISSES 83
COMTÉ 85
BRILLAT-SAVARIN 87
SMOKEY BLUE 89
STILTON 91
PICO PICANDINE 93
FUZZY WHEEL 95

CHEESE		BEER	
BLEATING HEART		FULL SAIL	
## Death & Taxes		## Session Lager	

country of origin	*alternatives*	*country of origin*	*other suggestions*
United States (California)	Four Fat Fowl St. Stephen	United States (Oregon)	Moonlight Brewing Company Moonlight Toast
family	Keswick Creamery The Stinky Elf	*style*	
Washed-rind		American lager	Brooklyn Brewery Brooklyn Lager
milk			
Cow			

ABOUT THE CHEESE: If you've ever driven north of San Francisco on Highway 101, perhaps you've had a chance to make a quick stop for a beer in Santa Rosa, and perhaps that beer was sipped at Moonlight Brewing, and perhaps that beer was the brewery's sweet and roasty Death & Taxes black lager. Forty or so miles away, Seana Doughty and Dave Dalton of Bleating Heart Cheese always have a keg of it on hand to wash the wheels of the exquisite semisoft cheese they named after the beer (and perhaps to partake in an after-work pint or two; who can say). The beer stains the rind the color of caramel corn, inflecting it with subtle cocoa sweetness under the funky cave aroma. Beneath that distinctive rind is a golden, buttery cheese with a supersmooth texture and the faintest inkling of sourness.

GOES BEST WITH: American lager. Tread carefully, reader. American lagers are by no small measure the most popular style of beer in the United States, but the market's choked with the output from such mega-conglomerates as Anheuser-Busch InBev and MillerCoors. While we admire the precision that goes into making every can of Budweiser taste exactly like the next can, these are not the beers we advocate drinking with cheese; they just don't bring enough to the table. Pale lagers, crafted on a much smaller scale by dedicated

brewers, showcase bready malts, palate-forward sweetness, gentle hoppiness, and a clean finish. They're bright, crisp, and sessionable (i.e., easily drinkable), perfect for warm summer days or washing down salty snacks.

Drinking a fine American lager with a wedge of Death & Taxes is to invite harmony into your life. Together they become one and the same, bolstering each other's most prominent qualities into a cohesive experience without losing any character in either the beer or the cheese. The well-salted Death & Taxes catches the beer's graininess and sugars, clarifying them until they evoke **cereal** and **honeycomb**. Meanwhile, the lager connects with the rind, bringing up those **cocoa** and **yeast** notes right alongside the beer's highlights while upping the cheese's creaminess to a decadent level.

QUICK BITE

The Family Tree of Cheese

All cheese starts out as milk, culture, and salt. Then, depending on how it's handled by the cheesemaker, it will fall into one of many categories on the cheese family tree. The largest branches on this tree include bloomy-rind (Brie, Camembert), washed-rind (Taleggio, Munster), blue (Stilton, Roquefort), Alpine (Comté, Gruyère), pasta filata (mozzarella, provolone), uncooked & pressed (Manchego, Gouda), milled-curd (Cheddar, Cheshire), and cooked & pressed (Parmigiano-Reggiano, Pecorino Sardo). Knowing that almost all cheeses fall into one of these families will make navigating a cheese counter much easier and a more pleasant experience.

CHEESE		BEER	
GRAFTON VILLAGE CHEESE ## Bear Hill		**PLZENSKY PRAZDROJ** ## Pilsner Urquell	

country of origin	*alternatives*	*country of origin*	*other suggestions*
United States (Vermont)	Hidden Springs Ocooch Mountain	Czech Republic	Radeberger Pilsner
			Victory Prima Pils
family	Lark's Meadow Farms Dulcinea	*style*	Urban Chestnut Stammtisch
Pyrenees-style washed-rind	Landmark Anabasque	Pilsner	
milk			
Sheep			

ABOUT THE CHEESE: The recipient of numerous well-deserved awards, Grafton Village Cheese's Bear Hill offers a rich, sweet, rouxlike creaminess accented with a light gamey presence that hints at a deeper complexity just waiting to be unearthed. Grafton's former master cheesemaker and passionate sheep's-milk cheese advocate Dane Huebner (now of Dane Huebner Cheese) created Bear Hill as a way to fill a void in the American market, a Vermonter's take on the Franco-Basque Ossau-Iraty (see page 143). Grafton Village Cheese holds a prominent position in Vermont's cheesemaking history, and the tale of its destruction by fire in 1912 and subsequent restoration in the 1960s by the nonprofit Windham Foundation to promote local dairies is an inspiring one. Fascinating provenance aside, the cheese speaks for itself.

GOES BEST WITH: Pilsner. Named for the Czech city of Pilsen, the straw-hued pilsner is a marvel held aloft to a summer sunbeam, and exponentially more satisfying the higher the mercury climbs. Pilsners, as do many light-colored lagers, seem straightforward and uncomplicated at first, but you can pick up a lot of fun aromas, such as violet petals and grain fields, if you can stop yourself from chugging it as soon as it hits your glass. The combination of pale malts, a touch of honey sweetness, and ample bite from the Noble hops practically screams "CRISP," a reputation we're happy to say pil-

sner upholds with gusto. Many Czech and German pilsners, packaged for some unfathomable reason in green bottles that permit too much light to penetrate the bottle, arrive in the United States tasting skunked, unfairly tainting many opinions of the style, so buy yours in brown bottles from a local brewer or get the overseas stuff in cans or on tap in a growler from a quality beer bar.

Pilsner's the ideal match for Bear Hill, because something really fun happens when you put them together: the beer becomes briney, complementing the creamy cheese and tricking your brain into thinking you're tucking into a bowl of fresh **clam chowder**. The pairing finishes with a big **herbal** note and a smidge of **lanolin**, that wool sweater flavor lingering throughout most sheep's milk cheeses. It's usually a distraction, but here it's a feature.

Noble Hops

Much like grapes, hops can be grown anywhere in the world the soil and climate will accept them, and their flavors and aromas will always vary based on their place of origin. Noble hops are the four varieties grown specifically in the German-Bohemian area of Europe: Hallertau, Saaz, Spalt, and Tettnang. You'll find them in every classic German and Czech ale and lager, such as pilsner, helles, bock, and weizen, where their earthy, spicy characteristics are cherished and held sacred. Got a bottle of Pilsner Urquell? Great example of a Saaz hop beer. Hofbräu Original? Hallertau, front and center. Plenty of American beers are made with US-grown versions of these hops, but no matter how authentic the recipe, they'll never taste *quite* like they would with hops from Deutschland.

CHEESE		BEER	
## Mimolette		REISSDORF ## Kölsch	
country of origin	*alternatives*		
France	Roth Prairie Sunset	*country of origin*	*other suggestions*
family	Pavé du Nord	Germany	Occidental Kölsch
Washed curd	Aged Edam	*style*	Champion Killer Kolsch
milk		Kölsch	Lancaster Kölsch
Cow			

ABOUT THE CHEESE: The French take on a Dutch cheese called Edam, Mimolette is one of the most visually striking cheeses you're ever going to find. On the outside, craters and pockmarks envelope this slightly squashed orb like a mini-moon, courtesy of some friendly little bugs (see the Quick Bite for more on that). Slice into it and you're greeted with an unforgettably deep, waxy orange the color of an electric-charged sweet potato. The bronze complexion comes courtesy of annatto, a natural food coloring used in such delicacies as *cochinita pibil* and Velveeta. While you can occasionally find younger, more delicate varieties of Mimolette, the aged version is more readily available, offering rich flavors of fatty meat and salted hazelnuts, with an undercurrent of fruitiness. One glance at it—inside or out—and you'll remember it for life.

GOES BEST WITH: Kölsch. Kölsch has created headache-inducing consternation among beer geeks who argue endlessly about whether it's an ale (because it's fermented with a specialized ale yeast) or a lager (because it's cold-conditioned, sometimes with lager yeast). We don't really care one way or the other; we drink it because we love the smooth marriage between up-front sweetness and a gentle hop bite in the crisp finish.

RESULTS

Layered on top of a nibble of Mimolette, Kölsch melds with the cheese's nuttiness and drops you straight into a **bucket of movie popcorn** with **tons of butter** poured over it, and maybe a little **butterscotch** in the bottom of the tub. In other words, a little slice of heaven for a butter lover.

QUICK BITE

Cheese Mites

What gives cheeses like Mimolette that craggy rind? Microscopic arthropods called cheese mites that feast on the fungi present on the outside of natural cheeses. Although essential to imparting the look and even a bit of the flavor to Mimolette, they're an incredible nuisance for other aged cheeses that can be irrevocably damaged by the burrowing bugs as they dig fissures and allow mold to penetrate past the rind. A cheese infested by the critters will be covered in a fine gray dust, a combination of the mites themselves and their feces that tireless cheesemakers usually wash, blow, or vacuum off regularly. Mimolette was even banned and quarantined in the United States from 2013 to 2014 by the FDA for fear the mites would cause allergic reactions in anyone deranged enough to eat the rind. All that fuss for something so small, yet so mighty.

Cheshire

GASTHAUS & GOSEBRAUEREI BAYERISCHER BAHNHOF
Leipziger Gose

country of origin	*other suggestions*
England	Wensleydale
	Lancashire
family	Sparkenhoe Red
Milled-curd	Leicester
milk	
Cow	

country of origin	*other suggestions*
Germany	Westbrook Gose
	Anderson Valley Gose
style	Off Color Troublesome
Gose	

ABOUT THE CHEESE: Poor Cheshire. Once one of England's favorite cheeses, Cheshire saw its popularity take a nosedive in the 1800s as competition from Cheddar and cheaper US factory-made cheese conspired to cut its market to a sliver of its former glory. The number of farms producing it dropped from around 2,000 to about 40 by the mid-1900s, pushing Cheshire closer to extinction, but the intervention of Neal's Yard Dairy, working with the Appleby family of cheesemakers to get Cheshire into shops across the globe, has resuscitated interest in this tangy, crumbly, pale orange treat. Originally, three distinct types of Cheshire existed based on the length of time its makers let it age, but the one we know and love today most closely resembles the Cheshires aged two to four months in the cheese's glory days. Some varieties have thin, sparse blue veins running through them, though this doesn't really affect the flavor, which somewhat resembles the acidic bite of cheese curds. A fantastic cheese for eating with fresh-picked apples and a bottle of something fizzy on a sunny autumn day.

GOES BEST WITH: Gose. If you've never tried sour beer before (no, we're not talking about good beer that's gone bad), Gose is a fine place to start. Pronounced "GO-zuh," Gose is cloudy yellow wheat ale originally brewed in Goslar, Germany, low in alcohol, lightly spiced with coriander, and famous for its bracing, lemony tartness tempered by a salty finish. Gose violates German's rigid Reinheitsgebot (see page 56), but it is still permitted as a regional specialty.

Gose's salinity keeps you thirsty for sip after sip, boosting the flavors of mildly salted cheeses like Cheshire. In this instance, the acidic cheese and the piquant beer find common ground and elevate each other for big **sweet-and-sour candy** flavors, specifically **Lemonheads** and **SweeTarts**, with **tart apple skin** thrown in for good measure.

QUICK BITE

Neal's Yard Dairy

Perhaps the United Kingdom's most prominent and important cheese retailer, Neal's Yard Dairy played an enormous role in the revival of Cheshire and other British farmhouse cheeses in the early 1980s. After purchasing the business in its first year, owner Randolph Hodgson quickly abandoned its original raison d'être of making yogurt and ice cream and shifted the focus to seeking out the highest-quality cheeses being made in Great Britain, which he then sold to the public. Hodgson had to compete with the supermarket juggernaut sweeping England with its inferior products sold at rock-bottom prices, but his dedication to farmhouse cheeses—especially those made with raw milk—carved out a niche for the company and established Neal's Yard as the British Isles' premier purveyor of world-class cheese. To this day it works closely with Britain's farmhouse cheesemakers, selecting cheeses and aging them at its maturation facility before sale. Neal's Yard Dairy's role as a key middleman in the supply chain between cheesemaker and consumer cannot be understated. No other company has come close to its fanatical promotion of small-farm cheeses, which has even led to the creation of brand-new cheeses, such as Stichelton, a raw milk version of Stilton. If you're ever in London, its shops in Covent Garden and Borough Market are must-visits.

CHEESE		BEER	

Fresh chèvre

BROUWERIJ VAN HOEGAARDEN
Hoegaarden Wit

country of origin	*alternatives*
France	Fromage blanc
family	Fresh brebis
Fresh	
milk	
Goat	

country of origin	*other suggestions*
Belgium	Allagash White
style	St. Bernardus Witbier
Witbier	Lost Coast Great White
	Celis White

ABOUT THE CHEESE: Although chèvre (French for "goat") can come young or aged, tart or mellow, fresh chèvre is a soft, spreadable cheese that retains the light acidity of goat's milk without a gut punch of tang. And we really do mean "fresh"— the variety of chèvre we're talking about can be ready to eat less than 24 hours after the milk comes out of the goat. Some cheesemakers introduce herbs into the chèvre, and while that's certainly a tasty way to enjoy this cheese, we suggest going for a clean, unadorned variety to keep it from clashing with your beverage.

GOES BEST WITH: Belgian witbier. We have a milkman to thank for every witbier we enjoy today. After the style was left for dead in 1957 when the last witbier brewery, Tomsin, closed in Belgium, a former worker at the brewery (who took up the milkman's trade in the aftermath) named Pierre Celis collaborated with another brewer to haul it back out of the grave.

RESULTS

Fresh chèvre was made for Belgian witbier (or just "wit"), a pale, cloudy, faintly sweet ale whose spices—typically coriander and curaçao orange peel—complement goat cheese's creamy blank canvas gorgeously. The sugars in the beer notch into the chèvre's mild tanginess like a sleek piece of gadgetry into its perfectly engineered case, a balanced contrast with a silky mouthfeel, all **candied oranges** and **passion fruit frosting**. This is such a great "gateway pairing" for people new to the concept of matching cheese with alcohol, not only because the flavors of the individual cheese and beer are so approachable, but because mashing them together creates something equally pleasant and harmonious.

QUICK BITE

Goats and Their Cheeses

Where would cheese be today without the hardy goat? As one of the first livestock animals to be domesticated (more than 10,000 years ago!), goats provided humans with their sweet, creamy milk long before cows became the dominant dairy animal. They're one of the most versatile creatures on the planet, requiring little land and able to eat almost anything you put in front of them. People usually associate "goat cheese" solely with fresh chèvre, but in actuality, goat cheeses are almost as varied as the animals themselves. Our favorites include Brabander (page 100), Garrotxa (page 159), Lorelei (page 55), Wabash Cannonball (page 154), and Dream Weaver (page 104). Listing every species of goat used to produce cheese would take more pages than we're willing to dedicate on the subject, so we'll call out some of the ones that most likely contributed to your favorite goat cheeses: Nubian, Saanan, French Alpine, Toggenburg, and LaMancha.

Torta del Casar

MYSTIC BREWERY
Mystic Saison

country of origin	*alternatives*
Spain	Ovelha
family	Lark's Meadow Farms Alto Valle
Thistle-renneted	
	Serra da Estrela
milk	
Sheep	

country of origin	*other suggestions*
United States (Massachusetts)	Blackberry Farm Summer Saison
style	Upright Pathways
Saison	Saison Dupont

ABOUT THE CHEESE: Hailing from the Portugal-adjacent Extremadura region of Spain (where Iberian ham comes from) and named for both the city of Casar de Cáceres and the fact that it's shaped like a cake or *torta*, the unique Torta del Casar is a protected designation of origin (PDO) cheese with a minimum of 50 percent fat in total solids and a maximum of 3 percent salt. It's usually served by slicing off the top bread-bowl style to gain access to the soft, spreadable paste, which tastes bright and tart like unripe strawberries, and a little bit like barnyard smells. You may even pick up a briny, herbaceous note from the thistle rennet used to coagulate the sheep's milk, and a yeasty aroma. Be careful pairing this one: many beverages—particularly beers—have a tendency to cloak Torta del Casar's more agreeable notes and bring out some rather unpleasant pasty flavors in their place.

GOES BEST WITH: Saison. A versatile style typically personified as light, highly carbonated ales with a pronounced yeast character, fruity esters, mild sweetness, and a dry finish, saisons are tough to nail down to rigid guidelines. The term *saison* (French for "season") is often used interchangeably with *farmhouse ale*, in that both are representative of the beers brewed at French and Belgian farms in the winter and consumed in the summer by the seasonal workers. Saisons have seen a recent surge in popularity after decades of

decline, thanks to the post-1990 brewery explosion, and its many interpretations can be found around the country with little effort.

What makes saisons work with the notoriously fickle Torta del Casar is the yeast: it locks arms with saison's farmhouse roots and dives headfirst into the funky cheese, generating a panoply of such flavors as **béchamel sauce** and **grapefruit peel**. We also picked up some of the spicier notes in the beer, especially **cloves**, which the cheese dug deep and drew out, all with the aforementioned **barnyard** aspects lingering in the background. The final package is so evocative of a farm, you may be suddenly overcome with the urge to go find some hay to thresh and a sheep to milk.

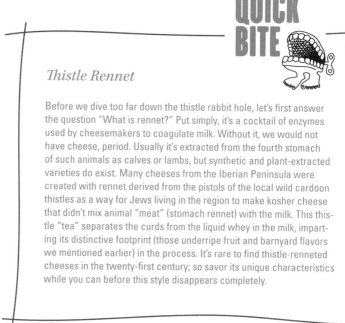

QUICK BITE

Thistle Rennet

Before we dive too far down the thistle rabbit hole, let's first answer the question "What is rennet?" Put simply, it's a cocktail of enzymes used by cheesemakers to coagulate milk. Without it, we would not have cheese, period. Usually it's extracted from the fourth stomach of such animals as calves or lambs, but synthetic and plant-extracted varieties do exist. Many cheeses from the Iberian Peninsula were created with rennet derived from the pistols of the local wild cardoon thistles as a way for Jews living in the region to make kosher cheese that didn't mix animal "meat" (stomach rennet) with the milk. This thistle "tea" separates the curds from the liquid whey in the milk, imparting its distinctive footprint (those underripe fruit and barnyard flavors we mentioned earlier) in the process. It's rare to find thistle-renneted cheeses in the twenty-first century; so savor its unique characteristics while you can before this style disappears completely.

BRIAR ROSE CREAMERY
Lorelei

country of origin	*alternative*
United States	La Fermière de Méan Cabricharme
family	Robiola
Washed-rind	Mont St. Francis
milk	
Goat	

SPATEN-FRANZISKANER-BRÄU
Franziskaner Hefeweizen

country of origin	*other suggestions*
Germany	Schneider Weisse
style	Live Oak
Hefeweizen	Bayern St. Wilbur Weizen

ABOUT THE CHEESE: In Dundee, Oregon, 45 minutes southwest of Portland, Sarah Marcus consistently delivers incredible cheeses, of which the World Cheese Award Gold Medal–winning Lorelei is but one of many delights. Smooth, graceful, with an understated goatiness that lacks any abrasive tang, you'd think it wouldn't stand a chance of holding its own with a flavorful drink. Ah, but you'd be wrong. The rind is washed in dark beer, which imparts a subtle fruitiness and maltiness to the cheese within. Lorelei has a knack for coaxing unexpected results from a companion beverage, softening hard edges and highlighting less prominent flavors that pair well with the cheese's intrinsic acidity.

GOES BEST WITH: German hefeweizen. Oh, what a difference the country of origin makes when picking out a good hefeweizen (*hefe* = "with yeast," and *weizen* = "wheat"). Whereas American wheat beers accentuate more hops and a broader range of flavors, German and German-style hefes strictly rely on fruity esters from specific yeasts that hammer you with BANANA, BANANA, BANANA, with fistfuls of cloves and bubblegum thrown in for good measure.

RESULTS

Although neither German hefe nor Lorelei comes from tropical climes, together they produce a lovely **coconut milk** flavor as the salt in the cheese balances out the sweetness of the beer. Think creamy **ambrosia salad**, that staple of American potlucks, and you're on the right track.

QUICK BITE

German Purity Laws

Back in 1516, Duke Wilhelm IV issued a string of decrees about the trade and regulation of Bavarian beer, largely to keep prices in check. A small component of this edict was an insistence that Bavarian lagers be made solely with water, malted barley, and hops; yeast was an assumed ingredient that was removed at the end of the brewing process. This had the twin benefits of retaining wheat for the breadmakers and protecting public health by forbidding potentially unhealthy additives. Fast-forward to the 1870s, when Germany unified and Wilhelm's law expanded to the rest of the country, minus the ingredient restrictions. Post–World War I, the restrictions returned, but only for lagers; ales, such as hefeweizens and goses, more common outside Bavaria, could continue to be brewed without sacrificing their more exotic ingredients. This is the version of the German purity law as we know it today, carrying the rather fearsome-sounding name of Reinheitsgebot.

CHEESE		BEER	

SHEPHERD'S WAY FARMS
Big Woods Blue

LINDEMANS
Cuvée René

country of origin	*alternatives*	*country of origin*	*other suggestions*
United States (Minnesota)	Bleu 1924	Belgium	The Bruery Rueuze
	Beenleigh Blue	*style*	Lost Abbey Duck Duck Gooze
family	Old Chatham Ewe's Blue	Gueuze	Oud Beersel Oud Gueuze Vieille
Blue			
milk			
Sheep			

ABOUT THE CHEESE: After suffering a devastating blow to the farm when a fire that killed most of its sheep and lambs and destroyed their housing in 2005, Shepherd's Way has made a miraculous comeback. Cofounders Jodi and Steven Read are producing some magnificent sheep's milk cheeses, none more so than Big Woods Blue. It's a bright, vanilla-sweet blue cheese balanced with a tangy, peppery pinch wherever the blue-green mold has taken hold, and an almondy finish.

GOES BEST WITH: Gueuze. If *gueuze* is a word that's never unfurled from your tongue, permit us a little direction: it's pronounced "gooz." A blend of young and old wild-fermented Belgian lambic beers, gueuze fully embraces the funk and the sour, hiding a labyrinth of flavors in every ounce (only natural given that it takes years to make this beer). Cracking open a bottle releases plumes of lemon, cherries, and musty cellars; not a bad preview of what's to come. On the palate, gueuze pops with citrus acidity, leading into horse blanket and leather, with an underlying bitterness. It's a borderline abrasive first sip, but once you adjust to the beer, you'll start picking out oak, earth, pears, grapefruit, and heaven knows what else.

RESULTS

With a funky blue cheese like Big Woods, it's only right to come at it with more funk, so a wild gueuze is just what the doctor ordered. At first, the cheese dials back gueuze's acid bite, producing smooth **buttermilk** flavors as a result. Then, the beer's citric tingle slowly regenerates, starting with **lemon curd on shortbread** and building into **salted limes** as the cheese asserts itself. Sweet, tart, salty, funky goodness all around.

QUICK BITE

Blue Cheese Basics

Blue is a broad umbrella for the family of cheeses that include such classics as Stilton, Roquefort, and Cabrales. But how does a blue cheese get blue? Most are born when *Penicillium roqueforti*, a fungus that occurs naturally underground, is added directly to liquid milk—cow's, goat's, or sheep's, it doesn't matter—before it coagulates and sets. A few days to a few weeks after the cheese has taken shape, it's stabbed repeatedly with long needles (surely a great release of stress for the individual doing the impaling) which create pathways for oxygen to reach the mold within. Duly fed, the mold blooms into tendrils of blue, green, gray, brown, or even black veins that spread through the cheese like rivers.

CHEESE		BEER	
Brie		BROUWERIJ BOON	
		Boon Kriek	
country of origin	*preferred bries*		
France	Pommier	*country of origin*	*other suggestions*
	Nangis	Belgium	St. Louis Kriek Fond Tradition
family	Jasper Hill Moses Sleeper	*style*	Drie Fonteinen Oude Kriek
Bloomy-rind		Kriek lambic	
milk			Firestone Walker Krieky Bones
Cow			

ABOUT THE CHEESE: The round, spreadable, soft-ripened cheese most associated with France, Brie is a revolution of complex flavors. Layers of cabbage, cauliflower, butter-sautéed mushrooms, and egg yolks somehow find coherence in the chaos, uniting into a decadent, fun foil for all manner of beverages. "Brie" has become a fairly broad catchall term for supple cheeses with luxuriously smooth textures, including the myriad bland American knockoffs masquerading as this abused style, so be sure to get yours from a reputable cheesemonger (if you don't have one locally, you have some great options to buy it online). One thing we want to point out: the rind is edible! It pains us deeply when someone carves out the innards of a wedge of Brie and discards the delicious outer shell. Don't be one of these people. And if you *are* one of these people, there's no time like the present to get your act together.

GOES BEST WITH: Kriek lambic. Sour beers, especially those aged on fruit in wooden barrels with wild yeast, have the potential for unparalleled complexity in aroma and flavor. You just never quite know what you're going to get at the end of fermentation. Brewers of sour ales have experimented with just about every fruit under the sun (Durian beer? Someone's made it, guaranteed) but kriek is the most

prevalent and popular. Ruby red from gobs of cherries—pits and all—a good kriek will strike a balance between tart and sweet, funky and familiar.

Stacking kriek on top of Brie is a one-way trip to the steakhouse. The cheese significantly cuts the beer's sweetness while the beer transforms the cheese's cabbage-and-broccoli act into a dead-on impression of **garlic butter** melted over a **juicy rib eye** sauced with **marchand de vin**. It's a meal!

QUICK BITE

True Lambic

The magic that is lambic beer starts when boiled wort (the sweet liquid produced after mashing grains with water) is exposed overnight in large, open, shallow metal vessels called coolships at the top of the brewery, where windows are vented to allow the wild yeasts and bacteria of Belgium's Senne River Valley to pour in. Once the wort has been inoculated, it's transferred into wooden barrels, which come loaded with their own cocktail of bacteria and yeasts, setting off a frothy fermentation and aging process that lasts from one to three years, or even longer in some cases.

All the while, the brewery's blender periodically tastes samples pulled from the barrels, determining how much of each to use in the finished product. Combining young lambics and adding candy sugar creates faro; blending young and old lambics produces gueuze; and adding fruit to the casks nets you fruit lambics, such as *kriek* (made with cherries), *peche* (peaches), or *framboise* (raspberries). Although no lambic will ever taste exactly like another, they all pack a wallop of funky, acidic aromas and flavors that, quite frankly, take some getting used to. But once you've become acclimated to lambic's eccentricities, they're positively transcendent.

CHEESE	BEER

Quadrello di Bufala

country of origin	*alternatives*
Italy	Bergamino di Bufala
family	La Maremmana
Washed-rind	Orossetano
milk	
Water buffalo	

BROUWERIJ VERHAEGHE

Duchesse de Bourgogne

country of origin	*other suggestions*
Belgium	Cuvée des Jacobins Rouge
style	Rodenbach Grand Cru
Flanders Red Ale	Pfriem Flanders Red

ABOUT THE CHEESE: Sticky and soft, with an aroma of mushrooms, your first taste of Quadrello di Bufala is going to leave a lasting impression, guaranteed. Essentially a buffalo milk version of Taleggio, Quadrello separates itself from the pack with the noticeable-but-not-overbearing triumvirate of funky, tangy, and yeasty flavors that characterize water buffalo dairy products. Definitely a picky cheese when it comes to pairing it with a beverage—don't even bother drinking German beers with it—so, look for something with a strong enough yeast flavor of its own to keep the Quadrello from pushing the needle too far into funktastic overdrive.

GOES BEST WITH: Flanders red ale. If you've never had a sour beer before, brace yourself: that first sip can really throw you for a loop. Get used to it, though, and the puckery smack can develop into an addiction that sends you searching for your next hit: see the current wild beer craze in the United States and the universal veneration for Belgian breweries, such as Rodenbach and Verhaeghe, as Exhibits A and B. Flanders red ale is a specific variety of sour beer made in the West Flanders region of Belgium. It's an acidic and tart, yet sorta-sweet treat packed with the flavors of raspberries, cherries, vanilla, prunes, and cola.

RESULTS

Flemish reds have enough backbone to tone down Quadrella's funk, while the cheese cuts the acid. Together they taste astonishingly close to **cherry cheesecake** and **blackberry tart**, a beautiful example of comparable flavors working in tandem.

QUICK BITE

Wild Yeasts

Single-celled fungi that exist in the air all around us and feed on sugars, fats, and proteins, wild yeasts play an important role in most kinds of fermentation, including beer, wine, cider, and even cheese. They give lambic beers their puckery punch, put the "sour" in sourdough bread, and colonize the surface of young cheeses, lowering the acidity to make a more inviting environment for flavor-producing bacteria. These yeasts can, if controlled properly, greatly benefit the finished product, adding a real "taste of place" to whatever they're devouring (it's why sourdough in San Francisco tastes different from sourdough in, say, Cleveland). If you see the word "Brett" on a bottle, as you're likely to do more often than not these days, that's *Brettanomyces*, a wild yeast so beloved for its barnyard, "horse blanket" flavors that it's actually commercially cultivated. *Saccharomyces* turns grape juice into wine, or apple juice into cider. Left unchecked, though, wild yeast can ruin the best cheese or beverage, turning malty beers lemony and cheeses inedibly gamy. Brewers and cheesemakers have learned to respect that which they cannot see, and keep their production facilities spic-and-span to ward off the threat of invasive species finding their way into the mix.

CHEESE		BEER	
CREAMERY 333		DOGFISH HEAD	
Trivium		**60 Minute IPA**	

country of origin	*alternatives*	*country of origin*	*other suggestions*
United States (Wisconsin)	Quicke's Goat Cheddar	United States (Delaware)	Stone IPA
	LaClare Evalon		Breakside IPA
family	Central Coast Goat Cheddar	*style*	Cigar City Jai Alai IPA
Cheddar (milled-curd)		India Pale Ale (IPA)	
milk			
Goat			

ABOUT THE CHEESE: As its name would suggest, everything about Trivium comes in triplets. The product of three collaborators, (a French affineur and the owners of Montchevre and Peterson Cheese, who dubbed themselves Creamery 333), Trivium puts a goaty spin on Cheddar, with three distinct waves of flavor packed into the alabaster cheese. The goat's milk is right up front, making its presence known with a measured tanginess that doesn't hit you over the head. Next comes a mellow earthy center with hints of roasted and salted nuts. Trivium concludes with a sweet finish reminiscent of malted milk and caramel that lingers long after the cheese has melted away. All three phases work in concert to present a cheese that is both evocative of Cheddar and yet unassailably different.

GOES BEST WITH: IPA. Ah, the IPA. So popular among beer geeks, so divisive among beer geeks. In the United States, India pale ale preferences have shifted away from the ultrabitter and toward the juicy, which has only improved the beverage as an accompaniment for cheese. While you can still track down massive hop bombs that decimate your palate, brewers are finding ways to appeal to broader audiences, namely by dry hopping their IPAs with mega-fruity hops to accentuate their flavor while keeping their bitterness in check. As

cheese-pairing beers, IPAs are always a major pain because hops tend to amplify flavors of whatever you eat with them, so funky, mold-forward cheeses are out of the question!

Luckily, some cheeses benefit from a little clumsy amplification. Take Trivium, for instance, whose every facet is interesting and worth taking a magnifying glass to. Trivium's tang and earthiness unite with an IPA's dank hoppy profile and end up tasting a lot like **salted asparagus**. After the earthy hit starts to fade, the salt in the cheese sweetens the beer just enough to line up with Trivium's goat's milk tang, finding some **Ruby Red grapefruit** common ground. A fun pairing that proves hops and cheese can coexist without strangling each other.

QUICK BITE

Dry Hopping

As brewers become more sophisticated and learn new techniques to enhance the flavor of their beers, one centuries-old practice continues to hold a permanent position in nearly every hop-centric recipe: dry hopping. This is the process of adding hops to a beer after it has finished fermenting, which infuses it with more hop aroma and flavor and less of the bitterness that comes when you introduce hops earlier. Nearly every IPA available is dry hopped, and the dry hopping method is even finding its way into ciders, meads, and other craft beverages. With the beer-drinking population's insatiable appetite for these dank aromas and flavors only growing, dry hopping is unlikely to disappear anytime soon.

CHEESE		BEER	

OLD CHATHAM SHEEPHERDING CO.
Nancy's Camembert

THE ALCHEMIST
Heady Topper

country of origin	*alternatives*	*country of origin*	*other suggestions*
United States (New York)	Shepherd's Way Hidden Falls	United States (Vermont)	Sierra Nevada Hazy Little Thing
family	Green Dirt Farm Ruby	*style*	Equilibrium Photon
Bloomy-rind	Perail de Brebis	New England–style IPA	Revision Disco Ninja
milk			
Sheep and cow			

ABOUT THE CHEESE: Named for Old Chatham Sheepherding Company cofounder Nancy Clark, Nancy's Camembert is an oddity of the cheese world worth tracking down. Although the physical resemblance to traditional Camembert (which we cover on page 170) can't be denied, the similarities end there: Nancy's version offers little in the way of pungency, and there are no audacious cabbage and garlic flavors to be found. In their place we have a much more restrained profile, mainly churned butter, hay, and mild acidity.

GOES BEST WITH: New England–style IPA. Likely the hottest trend to hit the beer scene the past few years has been the sudden ascension of the hazy IPA, a style that first appeared in Vermont in 2003 and has since spread like wildfire across the country. By making extensive use of dry hopping, incorporating particularly cloudy yeasts and/or high-protein grains (even flour!), then leaving the finished beer unfiltered, brewers concoct IPAs so juicy you'd swear someone had crushed orange, pineapple, guava, and passion fruit into the mix. Some may exhibit a dry, pithlike finish, but the vast majority prefer to zero in on hop flavor versus hop bitterness.

RESULTS A thick-bodied New England–style IPA and the creamy Nancy's Camembert quickly join forces to coat your mouth in a satiny smooth **Orange Julius**–like fruitiness that's simply joyful to experience. Then, the cheese's rind comes into play, and something really interesting happens: the beer coaxes out a hunky **panfried steak** note that ends the pairing in a completely different place than when it started. Fascinating stuff.

QUICK BITE

Ales vs. Lagers

Beer can be divided into one of two categories—ales and lagers—entirely dependent on the type of yeast used. On the technical side of things, ales are made with a yeast that sits near the top of the fermentation tank and activates at warmer temperatures, and lagers are fermented colder, with the yeast settling at the bottom. What does this mean for the finished beer? Ales, by far the older of the two styles, tend to embody bigger flavors and an underlying fruitiness known as esters: think pale ales, hefeweizens, ambers, and porters. Lagers, undergoing long, low-temp fermentation, end up with cleaner, crisper, brighter flavors: these are your pilsners, your bocks, and the vast majority of mass-market beer.

Research has shown that lager yeast, which only entered the scene as recently as the fifteenth century, actually originated as a wild yeast in South America's Patagonia region of all places, and likely hopped a ship to Europe just as transatlantic trade was taking off. Once it reached Bavaria, it hooked up with strains of ale yeast to form a new hybrid capable of tolerating colder conditions. And that's the same strain brewers use today!

Mahon Reserva

FULLER'S
Fuller's ESB

country of origin	*alternatives*
Spain	Matos St. George
family	Cobb Hill Ascutney Mountain
Pressed and uncooked	São Jorge
milk	
Cow	

country of origin	*other suggestions*
England	Yards Extra Special Ale
style	3 Floyds Lord Rear Admiral
ESB	Left Hand Sawtooth

ABOUT THE CHEESE: Hop a boat off Spain's east coast and eventually you'll reach the Balearic Islands sitting pretty as a picture in the aquamarine waters of the Mediterranean. Skip past crowded holiday destination Majorca to find its smaller and less famous sibling, Menorca, the exclusive home to Mahon cheese, rivaled only by Manchego in Spanish popularity. Records indicate the cheese has been made on the island since at least the fifth century, but its production boomed in the eighteenth century thanks to the British occupation of the island at the time. Young Mahon is soft and mildly salty, but aged Mahon, or Mahon Reserva, is pure butterscotch. It's a beautiful marriage of sweet and savory, like candied hazelnuts and beef broth, and a killer match for a beverage on the sweeter side.

GOES BEST WITH: ESB. ESB stands for "extra special bitter," which is kind of a misnomer: ESBs aren't particularly bitter at all. Instead, these English pale ales tend to let the sweet malts sit front and center, with a balanced application of hops to prevent tipping the scales too far into syrup territory. A good ESB will taste of caramel and biscuits, finishing crisp to keep your palate clean. ESB ranks the strongest in ABV (alcohol by volume) of the varieties of classic English bitters, which range from special bitter down to ordinary bitter. All should be given time to warm up if you're pulling them straight from the fridge.

RESULTS

ESBs already embody the essence of butterscotch, which make them the perfect fit for a nice hunk of buttery Mahon Reserva. Stacked on top of each other, the butterscotch becomes **butter rum**, with a big hit of **salted caramel**. Remember the old timey almond-bits-in-taffy candy **Bit-O-Honey**? Plenty of that here as well. The salty Mahon keeps the sweetness in check throughout, so balance is maintained at all times.

QUICK BITE

Real Ale

The term *real ale* entered the British beer-lover's vernacular in the 1970s when the Campaign for Real Ale, or CAMRA, launched a countermovement to the bland, heavily carbonated, mass-produced beers dominating the market. By CAMRA's estimate, a "real ale" (or cider, or perry) is a traditionally produced draft beverage that finished fermenting and conditioning inside whatever vessel from which it would eventually be dispensed (typically a cask or bottle), without any additional carbonation or additives. These ales must be served at cellar temperature, using a hand pump or simply gravity when poured, and they're known for a depth of flavor many feel is filtered or pasteurized out of commercially produced beers in favor of longer shelf life.

Although CAMRA's help enacted some real change in England with regard to preserving pubs and reducing excise duties, it's also endured ridicule for its erudite stances, poorly researched beer histories in its annual Good Beer Guide, and long dismissal of lagers. As of this writing, CAMRA is considering expanding its definition of what constitutes a "real" ale, cider, or perry with the goal of broadening its base, but only time will tell if the organization becomes more inclusive or adheres stubbornly (or resolutely, depending on how you look at it) to its original doctrines.

CHEESE		BEER	

CANAL JUNCTION
Charloe

BEAR REPUBLIC BREWING CO.
Red Rocket Ale

country of origin	*alternatives*	*country of origin*	*other suggestions*
United States (Ohio)	Consider Bardwell Farm Dorset	United States (California)	Switchback Ale
family	Gubbeen	*style*	Sixpoint Global Warmer
Washed-rind	Durrus	Red ale	Pipeworks Blood of the Unicorn
milk			
Cow			

ABOUT THE CHEESE: Other states, like Wisconsin and Vermont, may get the majority of the dairy-related attention in the United States, but Ohio has a beautiful portfolio of cheeses from such producers as Canal Junction, a nearly 170-year-old farmstead that only took up cheesemaking in 2007. The farm's award-winning Charloe smells strongly of roasted peanuts and pungent forest undergrowth, but the flavors hiding beneath that spotty orange rind are more tempered, leaning heavily on salted butter and beef broth. A great choice to introduce someone to washed-rind cheeses.

GOES BEST WITH: Red ale. Red ales (often lumped together with amber ales) are a stalwartly "middle-of-the-road" beer and still exist as a catchall for several styles, including ambers, red IPAs, Irish reds, double reds, etc. They attempt to strike a balance between hoppy and malty, bitter and sweet, and finding that perfect sliver in the center is no simple feat. Not many brewers pull it off successfully. The recent trend has been to push reds deeper into the hoppy/bitter end of the pool, but you'll still find plenty of examples that swing the other way, often embodying the essence of red licorice, with just a dash of hops to keep them from being cloying.

RESULTS

Because the typical red ale keeps both the malt and the hops from going wild, the simplified result ends up being a cracking good symbiotic match for Charloe. The cheese's meatiness acts as a pitch-perfect counterpoint to the malts in the beer, toning them down (especially if you're working with a sweeter red) without squashing them completely. Even better, the beer enlivens Charloe's saltiness, which makes it taste uncannily like a certain **crunchy cheese snack** with a cheetah for a mascot.

QUICK BITE

Farmstead/Farmhouse and Terroir

When you see the term *farmstead* or *farmhouse* applied to a cheese or beverage, it's referring to the fact that the product was made on an actual farm (caveat emptor: beware of "farmhouse-*style*" products, which are typically mass-produced goods artificially flavored or altered to taste more unrefined, as if that alone signifies something created on a farm). Many people (and that includes the two of us) are of the opinion that small-operation farmsteads imbue the very essence of their location into their products; this concept is known as *terroir.* An area's water, soil, wild yeast, climate, and local flora can all contribute to a farm's terroir and subtly change the flavors in a cheese, beer, wine, or cider made there, imparting a rusticity and inimitable sense of place.

CHEESE		BEER	
BOXCARR **Nimble**		**PAULANER** **Oktoberfest Märzen**	
country of origin United States (North Carolina)	*alternatives* Meadow Creek Grayson	*country of origin* Germany	*other suggestions* Urban Chestnut Oachkatzlschwoaf
family Washed-rind	Sleight Farm Cardo Alemar Cheese Good Thunder	*style* Märzen/Oktoberfest	Ninkase Oktoberfest Thomas Creek Octoberfest Lager
milk Cow and goat			

ABOUT THE CHEESE: A newer cheese on the scene, Nimble is the mixed-milk take on Boxcarr Handmade Cheese's own Lissom, striking to behold with a salmon-colored rind inlaid with tight parallel lines like a freshly iced pastry. Not only is the rind washed with beer, but dark ale from nearby Mystery Brewing ends up in the cheese itself, infusing it with a subtle maltiness that provides a nice foil to the more overt savory beef flavors. Like Taleggio, the cheese Lissom (and by extension, Nimble) was inspired by, it finishes with a playful twist of barnyard funk that coaxes you into taking just one more bite. Then another. And another . . .

GOES BEST WITH: Märzen/Oktoberfest. Long before the advent of electric refrigeration, Bavarian brewers had to sit out the hot summer months. That meant brewing lagers like Märzen ("März" is German for "March") in spring and storing them (often underground) until cooler weather returned in autumn post-harvest, when the changing season and subsequent Oktoberfest celebration meant breaking them out and reveling in their sweetness. They range from pale yellow to deep copper and make judicious use of roasted Vienna and Munich malts that impart luscious caramel and grainy cereal overtones, finishing crisp with a sorghumlike kiss.

Nimble's barnyard funk backs way off once a Märzen hits your palate. The cheese takes hold of the sweetness in the beer and thrusts it topside, riding those sugars deep into **butterscotch** territory. After the initial sweet smack wears off, the cheese slowly asserts itself, introducing flavors of **coconut** and **salted almonds** before a savory flash of **onion** and **beef** closes things out.

Oktoberfest

Oktoberfest is more than just a style of beer—it's an event. In October 1810, to celebrate the marriage of Prince Ludwig to Princess Therese, the city of Munich held a festival on the fields outside one of the city gates, with every citizen invited to join the fun. The festivities and particularly the horse races held at that first celebration were so popular that a second Oktoberfest the following year was an absolute must. Thus the tradition was born, getting bigger every year (except when the occasional war deigned to intervene).

Oktoberfest's main attraction has gradually shifted to the copious drinking the festival encourages, with great halls packed to the gills with raucous guests (Munich draws over six million visitors each Oktoberfest) and dirndled waitresses hefting several liters of beer in each arm. The only beer that can be served at the Munich Oktoberfest must be brewed by one of its six breweries: Augustiner, Hacker Pschorr, Hofbräu, Löwenbräu, Paulaner, and Spaten, and it must meet Reinheitsgebot requirements (see page 56). Smaller Oktoberfest celebrations have popped up all over the world with much more lenient restrictions, but the granddaddy of them all is worth experiencing at least once in your life, if you're able.

CHEESE		BEER	
MT. TOWNSEND CREAMERY		ABITA BREWING CO.	
## Off Kilter		## Turbodog	
country of origin	*alternative*	*country of origin*	*other suggestions*
United States (Washington)	Bleating Heart Death & Taxes	United States (Louisiana)	AleSmith Nut Brown Ale
family	Chimay	*style*	Samuel Smith's Nut Brown Ale
Washed-rind		Brown Ale	
milk			Midnight Sun Kodiak
Cow			

ABOUT THE CHEESE: If you ever get a chance to visit the town of Port Townsend, Washington, we recommend taking it. Overlooking Puget Sound, it's a quaint, quiet hamlet in the northeast corner of the Olympic Peninsula, full of some lovely old architecture (check out that old post office on the hill!) and, of course, Mt. Townsend Creamery. Off Kilter is a small, soft-ripened cheese with a musty aroma and satisfying fudgy texture hiding inside a wrinkly white rind made slightly sweet from its wash in Pike Brewing Company's Kilt Lifter Scotch Ale. Flavors here are subtle: a little chuck roast here, a hint of morels there, and a mild tang and earthy funk lingering on your tongue at the end.

GOES BEST WITH: Brown ale. Brown ale? Very underrated. Although often totally ignored by aficionados for being too middle-of-the-road, too unchallenging, it's a great food beer, with its malty sweetness, nutty overtones, and low, earthy hop profile pairing well with everything from roasted vegetables to a fat steak—and cheese. Brown ales aren't here to lay waste to your palate or get you drunk after sipping a few ounces; they're the unassuming friend who never asks too much of you and never offends anyone, but is always there when you need them.

RESULTS

Matched with something creamy, like Off Kilter, the combo shouts loud and clear: nut-studded baked goods, such as **brownies** or **chocolate chip cookies with walnuts**. The sweeter the beer, the further into dessert territory you'll go; take a bite of Off Kilter with a swig of ultrasweet Abita Turbodog and it's as if you've just bit off the end of a **Snickers bar**.

CHEESE		BEER	
KIRKHAM'S		**AECHT SCHERLENKA**	
# Lancashire		# Rauchbier Eiche	

country of origin	*alternatives*	*country of origin*	*other suggestions*
England	Caerphilly	Germany	Jack's Abbey
	Wensleydale		Smoke & Dagger
family		*style*	Surly Brewing Smoke
Milled-curd		Smoked beer/	Jester King
		Rauchbier	Viking Metal
milk			
Cow			

ABOUT THE CHEESE: Allow us a moment to lament the industrialization of Lancashire. The dry, crumbly, mildly acidic cheese most Brits now identify as Lancashire sprouted only as recently as the 1950s. Prior to that, Lancashire was a farmhouse cheese through and through, produced slowly due to lower supplies of milk. The cheesemaker would add rennet to the day's milk, let it curdle, then cut, press, and break the curd by hand. After repeating the process over several days, the funkier older and milkier newer curds were combined, creating a soft cheese that firmed and picked up more grassy notes as it aged. Some cheesemakers still produce Lancashire this way—you may see it labeled as "Tasty."

GOES BEST WITH: Rauchbier. One of the most polarizing beers around, rauchbier says "Auf Wiedersehen!" to subtlety and zeroes in on one gigantic, unrelenting flavor: smoke. That comes courtesy of smoked malt, traditionally dried over an open beechwood fire. A sorghum sweetness does manage to poke its head up once your palate adjusts, but teriyaki sauce and bacon reign supreme over all else.

RESULTS

Pairing Lancashire with a beverage is, we discovered, counterintuitive. We naturally assumed a cheese with as delicate a constitution as Lancashire would require a tactfully mild beverage, such as a semisweet cider or light farmhouse ale. Turns out what it really needs is something potent to latch onto, something it can support and push to the next level. And that something is rauchbier. Lancashire turns this liquid campfire into **hearty smoked brisket** and **beef jerky**, amplifying the beefiness so loud you can almost hear the cowbell. Astonishingly, the cheese starts pulling past the beer toward the finish, doling out **peat** and rich **butterscotch** flavors along with **salt** and **hay**. It shouldn't work, but by god it does.

CHEESE		BEER	

Aged Cheddar

MELVIN BREWING
2×4 Double IPA

country of origin	*preferred brands*		
England	Hook's	*country of origin*	*other suggestions*
	Shelburne Farms	United States	Green Flash
family		(Wyoming)	West Coast
Milled-curd	Milton Creamery		Fiddlehead
	Prairie Breeze	*style*	Second Fiddle
milk		Double IPA	
Cow			Southern Swells
			Truth Juice

ABOUT THE CHEESE: Synonymous with *cheese* for many, über-popular Cheddar's gotten a bad rap in America, thanks in no small part to cheesemakers great and small producing bland, one-note versions on the cheap in neon orange blocks. But look past the near-glowing supermarket stuff and you'll find Cheddars ranging from sweet and acidic to earthy and bitter, crafted by the likes of Fiscalini in California or Jamie Montgomery in Somerset, England. It's important to note that Cheddars can look and taste *wildly* different from one creamery to the next (see the Quick Bite for more), but we prefer ones made with raw milk and well aged (we're talking 18 months to 10 years). Great Cheddars offer marvelous complexity, sneaking in hints of horseradish, chives, and onion broth in varying degrees, depending on the age of what you buy and which creamery made it. Even the mass-market Cheddars have something to offer if you go with an extra-sharp variety.

GOES BEST WITH: Double India pale ale. Double IPAs, sometimes known as imperial IPAs or IIPAs, ratchet up everything that makes an IPA an IPA, which means more hops, more malts, more body, and more alcohol. A decade ago it might have meant more bitterness as well, but the modern

practice is to increase hop character (with fragrant hop aromas and straight-off-the-vine hop flavor) while reducing the tongue-lashing bitterness of IPAs and IIPAs of yore.

You'll want a good strong Cheddar to stand toe to toe with a double IPA's massive dank presence. You'll know you've found a good match when the beer and cheese manage not to cancel each other out, with the IIPA highlighting the sugars in the Cheddar and the Cheddar mingling with the hops in a blissful **umami-and-Brussels-sprouts** union.

QUICK BITE

The New Cheddar

Cheddar's come a long, long way from its roots in southwest England, so much so that most of today's Cheddars bear practically no resemblance to the original farmhouse varieties from days of yore. Bound in cloth and aged at room temperatures—and thus exposed to molds in the open air—these early Cheddars developed tangy, bitter, oniony flavors with a lot of bite. With the advent of coating cheese in wax to protect it from the elements, Cheddar began to take on nuttier, fruitier notes, often with crunchy little amino acid nuggets.

Then, in the 1990s, everything changed again. Cheesemakers started introducing *Lactobacillus* bacteria (normally used in Alpine and Swiss cheeses) into their Cheddars to smooth out the sharpness, resulting in creamier, much sweeter cheeses that appealed to a greater range of palates. This style dominates the American Cheddar scene at the moment, but if you want a taste of the old stuff, seek out a wedge of Montgomery's Cheddar from Neal's Yard Dairy. The difference between that and, say, a big block of something from your supermarket's cold case, will leave you scratching your head at how they could both possibly be called Cheddar.

CHEESE		BEER	
Époisses		WEIHENSTEPHANER **Korbinian**	
country of origin	*alternatives*		
France	Soumaintrain	*country of origin*	*other suggestions*
	Limburger	Germany	Spaten Optimator
family	Forsterkase		Capital Autumnal Fire
Washed-rind		*style*	Paulaner Salvator
		Doppelbock	
milk			
Cow			

ABOUT THE CHEESE: The definitive stinky French cheese. First produced by monks centuries ago at the Abbaye de Citeaux in Burgundy, Époisses was nearly abandoned when World War II swept through France, but then the Berthaut family rescued it from extinction in the 1950s and almost singlehandedly returned it to its rightful prominence. The cheese itself isn't the bacchanalian funk-fest its notoriously pungent red-orange rind would have you believe it to be, but brought to room temperature it will ooze with garlicky, bacony umami flavor and spread like frosting on the back of a spoon. Talk about character.

GOES BEST WITH: Doppelbock. If you have an aversion to hops but love malt, a doppelbock is just what the doctor ordered. This German lager pours a dark copper and gives off an aroma of prunes and dark chocolate, both of which turn up again when the beer hits your palate. Unlike porters or stouts, doppelbocks aren't roasty; instead they rely on clean malt sweetness, which to be fair has been toned down somewhat since they were first brewed by Bavarian monks as a less alcoholic, more breadlike beer. Even so, this is still a sweet flavor bomb, packing caramel, sorghum, and toffee into every ounce.

Époisses and doppelbock is a BIG + BIG equation in which neither side gives up an inch of its territory, both acting as a brilliant contrast to the other. Époisses doesn't diminish the doppelbock's **caramel sweetness** in the slightest, but it provides a **meaty counterpoint** that helps stave off palate fatigue from all that sugar. And the beer, so flavorful but so accessible, gives the challenging-for-some Époisses an entry point that eases you into its rich, funky world.

QUICK BITE

Doppelbock: The Godly Beer

Imagine giving up solid food for 46 days. Could you do it? Bavarian Catholic monks undertook this sacred challenge every year for Lent, but in the seventeenth century, the Paulaner monks of the Cloister Neudeck ob der Au devised an ingenious way to keep some calories and carbohydrates flowing during the long fast while sticking to a liquid-only diet: brewing beer. A new beer called *Doppelbock*, to be precise, which they named Salvator.

For decades the monks subsided on this "liquid bread" during Lent, until, worried the beer was too delicious to consume during what was supposed to be a time of sacrifice, they sent a keg to the pope in Rome to get his official thumbs-up. We'll never know whether the pontiff would have given his approval to *Doppelbock* as the monks knew it, because by the time the keg reached him, the beer had spoiled and was so vile he deemed it more than acceptable as Lenten sustenance. Papal blessing: acquired!

CHEESE		BEER	

Comté

BRASSERIE DE ROCHEFORT

Trappistes Rochefort 6

country of origin	*alternatives*		
France	Gruyère	*country of origin*	*other suggestions*
family	Beaufort	Belgium	Chimay Première
Pressed and cooked	Challerhocker	*style*	Elm City Abbey Dubbel
milk		Dubbel	Westmalle Trappist Dubbel
Cow			

ABOUT THE CHEESE: Comté has a lot of rules it must adhere to if it even wants to be called Comté. To meet its fancy appellation d'origine contrôlée (AOC; see Quick Bite) and protected designation of origin certifications, it must be from France's Massif du Jura region, made from the milk of French Simmental or Montbéliarde cows fed non-GMO grass and hay, and made no farther than 16 miles from where the cows were milked. (There's more, but we'll leave it at that.) Expect a deep earthiness to the flavor, like mushrooms cooked in browned butter, with a hint of sweetness. A staple of any self-respecting cheesemonger!

GOES BEST WITH: Dubbel. One of the classic abbey ales or Trappist beers (named as such for the proliferation of monks brewing them), the Belgian dubbel (Flemish for "double") is a malty, sweet, sometimes fruity brown beer with a rich body and some hops thrown in for bitterness. The color comes from highly caramelized candi sugar, which imparts a lighter roast. To allow the flavors in a dubbel to really come to life, take it out of the fridge 20 to 30 minutes before you plan to drink it.

RESULTS Because Comté isn't a salt bomb like some cheeses, it allows dubbel to take it into the magical bittersweet dessert realm of **hot fudge** and **brownies, marzipan** and **dark chocolate**. One for the chocoholic in all of us.

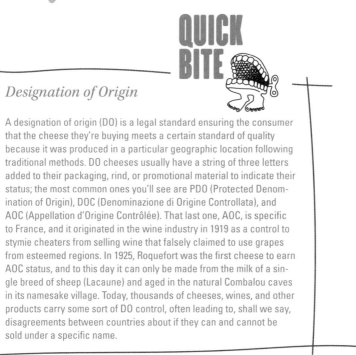

QUICK BITE

Designation of Origin

A designation of origin (DO) is a legal standard ensuring the consumer that the cheese they're buying meets a certain standard of quality because it was produced in a particular geographic location following traditional methods. DO cheeses usually have a string of three letters added to their packaging, rind, or promotional material to indicate their status; the most common ones you'll see are PDO (Protected Denomination of Origin), DOC (Denominazione di Origine Controllata), and AOC (Appellation d'Origine Contrôlée). That last one, AOC, is specific to France, and it originated in the wine industry in 1919 as a control to stymie cheaters from selling wine that falsely claimed to use grapes from esteemed regions. In 1925, Roquefort was the first cheese to earn AOC status, and to this day it can only be made from the milk of a single breed of sheep (Lacaune) and aged in the natural Combalou caves in its namesake village. Today, thousands of cheeses, wines, and other products carry some sort of DO control, often leading to, shall we say, disagreements between countries about if they can and cannot be sold under a specific name.

Brillat-Savarin

FOUNDERS BREWING CO.
Dirty Bastard

country of origin	*alternative*	*country of origin*	*other suggestions*
French	Cowgirl Creamery Mt. Tam	United States (Michigan)	Belhaven Wee Heavy
family	Explorateur		Great Divide Claymore
Bloomy-rind	Tulip Tree Trilium	*style*	Alesmith Wee Heavy
milk		Scotch ale	
Cow			

ABOUT THE CHEESE: In the world of triple-crèmes, few hold as much cachet as Brillat-Savarin. Named for a legendary eighteenth-century politician and food writer who compared a dinner without cheese to a woman with only one eye, Brillat-Savarin boasts a butterfat content of 75 percent and a soft white rind housing a paste so delicate it practically oozes out at the touch of a blade once it reaches room temperature. What does such an indulgence taste like? Chanterelles and butter, but slightly sour and musty. Made by a trio of dairies in the Île de France region, it's readily available in cheese shops across the United States and elsewhere, so experiencing its luxuriously silky mouthfeel shouldn't be too difficult.

GOES BEST WITH: Scotch ale. Sometimes called a "Wee Heavy," the Scotch ale is all about the caramel. Typically a higher-alcohol beer due in part to the caramelization of the wort during the brewing process, you can expect candylike sweetness, peripheral bitterness, and some alcohol burn. Perfect for a chilly night in the Scottish highlands, or someplace closer to home.

RESULTS

Take a swallow with a bit of Brillat-Savarin *without* the rind and you'll taste a **root beer float** with **vanilla ice cream**. *With* the rind, the beer amplifies the cheese's fungal qualities, recalling **mushrooms sautéed in sweet wine**. Either way, it's a great combination to show your friends just how much fun beer and cheese can have together.

QUICK BITE

Triple-crème

Triple-crèmes are all about injecting decadent levels of fat into cheese to get it as smooth and velvety as possible. This is accomplished by adding cream to the milk, pushing the butterfat-in-dry-matter content to at least a whopping 75 percent. These cheeses focus squarely on creamy, delicate textures and richness rather than depth of flavor. In this regard, an easy way to think about them is butter with a bloomy rind.

CHEESE		BEER	
ROGUE CREAMERY **Smokey Blue**		DESCHUTES BREWERY **Black Butte Porter**	
country of origin United States (Oregon) *family* Blue *milk* Cow	*alternative* Roth Moody Blue Caves of Faribault AmaBlue	*country of origin* United States (Oregon) *style* Porter	*other suggestions* Smuttynose Robust Porter Edmund Fitzgerald Porter Odell Cutthroat Porter

ABOUT THE CHEESE: Proclaimed the world's first smoked blue cheese, the Smokey Blue from southern Oregon's Rogue Creamery is both a visual stunner and a roundhouse kick to the palate. Blue-green pockets share real estate with long, ruler-straight tracts of mold where stainless-steel needles impaled the ivory cheese to promote its growth. Cold-smoked over Oregon hazelnut shells, it's bitingly sharp yet pleasantly sweet, reminiscent of bacon and honey. Such a powerful cheese is not to be toyed with when it comes to pairing; avoid lighter beers, wines, and ciders altogether and stick with something with a lot of body and flavor. Everything else is going to get dominated by this beast.

GOES BEST WITH: Porter. Many people inaccurately correlate dark beer with high alcohol, but despite their motor oil complexion, most porters fall neatly into the 5 to 6% ABV spectrum. The difference between porters and stouts is a murky one at best, and we're not going to write a dissertation on the subject; if it says "porter" on the label, it will suffice for this pairing (unless preceded by the word "Baltic," which is different enough to warrant mentioning). Porters range from dry and bitter to sweet and chocolaty, all with a decently roasty backbone akin to black coffee or burnt toast.

RESULTS

Porter's the perfect accompaniment to Rogue Creamery Smokey Blue. The toasty notes in the beer and the smoke permeating every pore of the cheese strongly evoke the flavors of the Pacific Northwest, specifically **fresh-roasted coffee** and **smoked salmon**. Pair the Smokey Blue with a porter from Oregon or Washington and you've got one of the best examples ever of how regional pairing can work wonders.

CHEESE		BEER	
COLSTON BASSETT		BELL'S BREWERY	
## Stilton		## Kalamazoo Stout	

country of origin	alternatives	country of origin	other suggestions
England	Shropshire Blue	United States (Michigan)	Fort George Cavatica
family	Jasper Hill Bayley Hazen Blue		New Holland Dragon's Milk
Blue	Cascadia Glacier Blue	style	Ballast Point The Commodore
milk		Stout	
Cow			

ABOUT THE CHEESE: One of the most famous blue cheeses in the world and certainly the most cherished in Britain, Stilton has phased through a few iterations since the early 1700s to reach its lofty modern status. Records indicate it was originally a hard cream cheese made with raw milk, not always blue, cooked and pressed and referred to by *Robinson Crusoe* author Daniel Defoe as the "English Parmesan." Gradually, standardized recipes and the advent of factory-produced cheese with pasteurized milk and mold cultures delivered a consistent product shot through with a network of blue veins and brimming with flavors of earth, cream, hay, grass, and especially roasted peanut shells. Dutiful research has determined that Stilton did not, in fact, originate in the town of Stilton, but in the nearby county of Leicestershire. Today, the cheese holds PDO status (see page 86) and can only be made in the counties of Leicestershire, Derbyshire, and Nottinghamshire. That means cheese made to the exact specifications as Stilton produced in the town of Stilton itself cannot be called Stilton (in that specific instance, the cheese is called Stichelton). Only six dairies supply the world with Stilton, and of those, the buttery, potent Colston Bassett is our favorite.

GOES BEST WITH: Stout. For those who find hops generally disagreeable and prefer their beer the color of fountain

pen ink, stout is the beverage of choice. Sometimes they're indistinguishable from their closest sibling, porter, though the general rule of thumb is that stouts are "more"; that is, more roasty, more chocolaty, more dark, more *more*. Usually brewed with malts or barley roasted until charred, stouts celebrate the joy of all things dark: burnt toast, coffee beans, and unsweetened cocoa, all laying down a backbone of moderate to heavy bitterness.

If you enjoy chocolate with peanut butter, then stout and Stilton go together about as well as any food and drink you're ever going to try. Stilton's peanutty overtones single out the cocoa flavors inherent in stouts (even ones made without cocoa) and taste like good-quality **peanut butter cups made with very dark chocolate**. As you start into the section of Stilton closest to the rind, the combo takes on a richer, earthier flavor that reminds us of **walnut liqueur**. There's something so calming and so deeply satisfying about this pairing that makes us just want to sink into a leather chair in front of a fire on a cold winter's day.

QUICK BITE

Malt Roasting

The roasting of malts acts almost the same way as the roasting of coffee beans, adding color, body, sweetness, or bitterness depending on how light or dark the roast is and whether the malts have been dried first. For example, caramel malts derived from germinated barley are "stewed" wet at high heat to crystallize the sugars, and then roasted, which allows those sugars to caramelize and add sweetness and body to beer. Roasting malts after they've been kiln-dried produces biscuit, brown, and chocolate malts, which add more color, toasty flavor, and bitterness to beer. Aspiring homebrewers can roast their own malt in their home oven; consult your friendly neighborhood internet for details if the idea strikes your fancy.

CHEESE		BEER

Pico Picandine

BIERBROUWERIJ DE KONINGSHOEVEN

La Trappe Quadrupel

country of origin	*alternatives*		
France	Creamery 333 Tricycle		
family	Andante Dairy	*country of origin*	*other suggestions*
Bloomy-rind	Acapella	Belgium	Rochefort 10
	Idyll Gris		Ommegang
milk		*style*	Three Philosophers
Goat		Quadrupel	Vivant Wizard
			Burial Ground

ABOUT THE CHEESE: Some cheeses excel at taking one distinct flavor and throwing everything they have behind it. Then there are cheeses that require a little more participation, cheeses that revel in subtlety and unfold slowly like a flower at daybreak. Pico is one of those cheeses. It's a goat's milk cheese (in case the drawing of goats on this cheese's cute little round wooden box didn't clue you in), so you'll get a little of that natural tang, but the funk is much more subdued than you might expect from a bloomy rind. Let a slice (room temperature, of course) linger on your palate and just wait for the notes of salted butter, yeast, hay, and minerals to stretch their legs.

GOES BEST WITH: Quadrupel. Despite their association with Trappist monks who have been brewing for ages, quadrupels, or quads, have only been around since the 1980s, when the La Trappe brewery switched from lagers to traditional monastic ales and invented a style along the way. The next step up from a Belgian dubbel or tripel, quads mean business and can knock you off your feet if you don't take them seriously. These are high-alcohol ales with a potent sweetness and a creamy mouthfeel, with lots of cola, licorice, fennel, almond extract, fig, and raisin character draped over an underlying roastiness.

RESULTS A Belgian quad brings Pico to life, lifting its sundry facets into a more visible layer. Unexpectedly, those delicate, mildly funky flavors—now amplified—don't clash with the burlier flavors in the beer, they complement them! You get more **goaty tang** out of the cheese, rising to the **licorice** notes in the beer and matching them equally. Quad's fig flavors mesh joyously with Pico's buttery profile, and the cheese's subtle **minerality** is pure magic with the beer's **cola** character.

QUICK BITE

Monastic Brewing

Monks have brewed for more than 1,500 years, but it was the northern European Trappist monks of the Cistercian order who put beer on the historical map. Along with farming, cheesemaking, bread baking, and charitable giving, brewing was a cornerstone of the Trappist tradition. Given the scarcity of potable water, beer was simply a safer liquid to drink, and monasteries brewed three: one to sell, one to drink themselves, and one to give to pilgrims and the poor.

Today, there are 11 recognized Trappist breweries in operation, all of them exalted by the beer-drinking community, including six in Belgium, two in the Netherlands, one in Italy, one in France, one in Austria, and even one in the United States (Spencer). All 11 adhere to the traditions of the past, and all produce world-class beer.

TWIG FARM
Fuzzy Wheel

country of origin	*alternatives*
United States (Vermont)	Tomme Crayeuse
	Sweet Grass Dairy
family	Thomasville Tomme
Natural rind	Saint-Nectaire
milk	
Goat and cow	

MAD RIVER BREWING
John Barleycorn Barleywine

country of origin	*other suggestions*
United States (California)	East End Gratitude
	Free State Old Backus
style	Perennial Vermilion
Barleywine	

ABOUT THE CHEESE: With an undulating, mold-covered rind resembling the surface of Jupiter and reeking of dog's breath, Fuzzy Wheel from Vermont's Twig Farm may not come across as particularly inviting at first glance (or sniff). But beneath its smelly, flocculent surface is an ivory cheese jam-packed with intriguing flavors that become more and more daring the longer it ages. An earthy nut butter kicks things off when the cheese hits your tongue, moving on to damp cellar and finally horseradish, with some hints of fresh milk and grass waving at you off in the distance.

GOES BEST WITH: Barleywine. Popping open a barleywine is always serious business. These boozy malt-and-hop bombs come loaded for bear with complex bittersweet flavors of molasses, dates, caramel, pine, and prunes, all predecessors to that hot alcohol finish. American versions are more aggressively hopped than their English counterparts, often jacking up the bitterness as a result, so try a few from each side of the pond to see which you prefer.

RESULTS

A flavorful cheese like Fuzzy Wheel calls for a flavorful beer, and barleywine is more than up to the challenge. That **horseradish**-like heat in the cheese shakes hands with barleywine's boozy burn and spreads like a gentle napalm over your palate, coating your mouth in an intoxicating warmth that turns to **toffee sweetness** as it slowly fades. This is a pairing to last you all night, best consumed in nibbles and sips.

CHEESE WITH WINE

CHEESE		WINE	
VERMONT CREAMERY		**PETIT ROYAL**	
# Cremont		# Lambert de Seyssel	
country of origin	*alternatives*	*country of origin*	*other suggestions*
United States (Vermont)	Pico Picandine	France	Domaine de Vens-le-Haut Seyssel Altesse
	Ruggle's Hill	*style*	
family	Ada's Honor	Seyssel	Maison Mollex Seyssel La Tacconniere
Double-cream, bloomy-rind	River's Edge		
	Sunset Bay		
milk			
Goat and cow, with cream			

ABOUT THE CHEESE: It started with a dinner. Bob Reese, the then-marketing director for the Vermont Department of Agriculture, needed a fresh chèvre for a state dinner showcasing local foods, and Allison Hooper, a state dairy lab tech, created it for him. Vermont Creamery was born, going on to accumulate accolades galore, including the World Cheese Award for Cremont, the "Cream of Vermont." This smooth, delicate cheese, as spreadable as room-temperature butter, waits within its brainlike wrinkled *Geotrichum* rind to entice you with a spectrum of flavors ranging from fresh milk to roasted nut shells, bolstered by pillars of citrus, yeast, and the telltale goat tang.

GOES BEST WITH: Seyssel. One of France's oldest wine appellations, Seyssel is named for a small village in the Savoie near the Swiss border. Seyssels are made entirely from some combination of Molette and Altesse grapes, which together produce a bright white wine with big floral, bready aromas and a deft balance between the sweetness of honey and the tart zing of a Granny Smith apple.

RESULTS

This pairing is all about taking a wine from one end of the pH scale and a cheese from the opposite end and finding a bridge between them. In this case, it's the yeast factor in both that spans the chasm. The yeasty aromas and flavors come through in a big way, with the acid of the Seyssel and the soothing creaminess of the Cremont blending effortlessly behind them to elevate the sweeter notes in the wine. With that prominent yeast presence, the effect is not unlike a **sweetened bread** or **breakfast pastry** that dances across your palate before washing away in a river of tiny bubbles.

QUICK BITE

American Cheese Society

An important player in the second coming of artisan cheese in the United States has been and continues to be the American Cheese Society (ACS). Formed in 1983 by Cornell University's Dr. Frank Kosikowski, a lifelong expert on cheese (and cofounder of the gloriously named American Cottage Cheese Institute), the ACS had a singular mission: to nurture small cheese producers, retailers, and enthusiasts, and foster growth in the fledgling industry. Since the '80s, the ACS has become a well-oiled machine that advocates for its members by lobbying for sensible regulation and expanding public awareness of talented cheesemakers and their handcrafted products.

At the ACS's annual convention, cheesemakers compete for prestigious awards that can give the winners a significant sales boost and well-deserved bragging rights. The most recent competition exceeded 2,000 entries from North through South America, and that number is only expected to grow as cheesemaking on this side of the globe continues to blossom.

CHEESE		WINE	

ESSEX ST. CHEESE
Brabander

country of origin	*alternatives*
Holland	Mekkerstee
family	Central Coast Goat Gouda
Gouda	Black Betty
milk	
Goat	

JACQUES LASSAIGNE
Les Vignes de Montgueux

country of origin	*other suggestions*
France	Delamotte Brut Blanc de Blancs
style	José Dhondt Brut Blanc de Blancs
Champagne Blanc de Blancs	

ABOUT THE CHEESE: Remember this name, Brabander, for one taste will leave you questioning the plausibility of a life without a fresh wedge of it forever occupying a corner of your refrigerator. Hailing from the Brabant region of Holland, south of Amsterdam, this pale cream-colored beauty is the secret weapon for any self-respecting cheese plate. It's surprisingly complex, offering sweet, milky flavors alongside a bright acidity and coconut-like undertones. Brabander is one of those can't-miss pairing cheeses, working ridiculously well with just about any beverage you throw at it, but it really blossoms with beers, wines, and ciders with palate-forward sugars, which draw out the cheese's butterscotch-and-caramel attributes. If you're ever unsure about which cheese to pair with a particular beverage, Brabander should be at the top of your list.

GOES BEST WITH: Champagne Blanc de Blancs. Blanc de Blancs ("white of whites") is a 100 percent Chardonnay Champagne, somewhat less common than the typical Champagne blend of Chardonnay, Pinot Noir, and Pinot Meunier grapes. So, what are the differences? For one, Blanc de Blancs often embody a tangible salinity, not unlike salted goses in the beer world. For another, they offer deeper, more complex flavors that highlight the herbal undertones of the grapes and their minerality, along with a brioche-like yeastiness. Lambic beer drinkers will be right at home with some of the funkier versions, such as the Jacques Lassaigne Les Vignes de Mont-gueux, which greets you with Greek yogurt on the nose and the sweet acidity of lemon curd.

Champagne Blanc de Blancs and Brabander is a match made in dessert heaven. Eat them together for an immediate **toasted marshmallow** sensation; it's uncanny how quickly this pairing transports you fireside with a lightly charred cube of gooey white sugar sliding off the pointed end of a stick into your mouth. Once you get past the marshmallow bomb, subtler flavors of **coconut cream pie** and fluffy **meringue** drizzled with **caramel** emerge to round things out. So much fun!

CHEESE		WINE	
Wrångebäck		GRUET FAMILY **Sauvage Rosé**	
country of origin	*alternatives*		
Sweden	Beaufort	*country of origin*	*other suggestions*
family	Comté	United States (New Mexico)	Langlois Crémant de Loire Rosé
Pressed and cooked Alpine style	Jasper Hill Farm Alpha Tolman	*style*	Domaine Tissot Crémant du Jura Rosé
milk		Sparkling rosé	
Cow			

ABOUT THE CHEESE: For centuries, monks have tended the 8,800-acre Almnäs Bruk farm in Skaraborg, Sweden, but it wasn't until the 1830s that they decided to add cheesemaking to their repertoire. In 1889, they invented and registered Wrångebäck, making it the oldest registered cheese brand in the country. The industrialization of cheese eventually shut down the farm's cheese operation in the 1960s, but in 2008, Almnäs brought back one of its former dairymen, Hans Stiller (now in his 80s!) to start making Wrångebäck again using the original recipe and the old dairy's original wooden aging planks, bacterial cultures, and all. The result is an Alpine-style cheese with some lovely savory flavors, namely stewed onions, pork fat, and mustard, with a touch of sweet Cheddar and a little funk.

GOES BEST WITH: Sparkling rosé. Rosé, that coral-hued libation of juice from red wine grapes left in contact with their pigment-loaded skins only until the proper color is attained, is more popular than ever. That's a good thing: it means the selection of high-quality rosés will only increase. The types of grapes used in the blend and how long those grapes are left to macerate on their skins greatly inform the flavors of individual rosés, and the differences can be dramatic. Most will showcase floral, occasionally piney aromas with tropical fruit flavors, such as guava or melon, lots of

strawberry and watermelon, and maybe with a little rhubarb thrown in if it's on the tart side. The bubbles in sparkling rosés act as a palate cleanser, allowing these wines to stand up to bolder cheeses you wouldn't necessarily want to pair with still rosés. Cheeses like Wrångebäck, for example.

Sparkling rosé and Wrångebäck is one of the wildest, most fun cheese-and-wine combinations you'll ever consume. When these two get together, a cornucopia of sweet and savory flavors come bursting out one after the other in rapid succession. We picked up everything from **dumplings**, **Brussels sprouts**, and **German potato salad** to **ham**, **pork belly**, and **strawberries**, each flavor coming so fast after the previous that we could barely write them down fast enough. You've got to try this combo; it's a complete picnic in every bite and sip.

QUICK BITE

Cows and Their Cheeses

Ayrshire, Holstein, Guernsey, Jersey, Brown Swiss, Montbéliarde . . . these are but a sliver of the cows with which cheesemakers form an essential partnership when crafting their cheeses. Each breed offers milk in different quantities, butterfat content, and protein levels, making the choice of which cow's milk will end up in any particular cheese one worth pondering over.

When it comes to sheer quantity of milk, Holstein reigns supreme. Need something richer and fattier? Jersey's your girl. Ayrshire provides a happy medium with decent milk yields and smaller fat molecules. If tradition is important, as with such AOC-designated cheeses as Comté, then Montbéliarde or Simmental is a must. Making a classic English Cheddar? The Innisfail Shorthorn is a good choice.

Cow's milk, which has been consumed by humans for at least the past 10,000 years, can be used to produce different cheeses so unlike one another that it's rather impressive they can all come from a single animal. Just look at the ones covered in this book: Wrångebäck is nothing like Death & Taxes is nothing like Cheddar is nothing like Harbison is nothing like Mimolette. With production often at surplus levels, we can only expect more exciting cow's milk cheeses to emerge from the next generation of brilliant cheesemakers!

CHEESE		WINE	
CENTRAL COAST		**CÀMAIOL**	
## Dream Weaver		## Sebastian Brut Rosé	
country of origin	*alternatives*	*country of origin*	*other suggestions*
United States (California)	La Fermière de Méan Cabricharme	Italy	Paltrinieri Radice Lambrusco di Sorbara
family	Capriole Mont St. Francis	*style* Sparkling brut rosato	Ferrari Brut Rosé
Washed-rind	Fromagerie Le Détour Sentinelle		
milk			
Goat			

ABOUT THE CHEESE: High school sweethearts Reggie and Kellie Jones opened Central Coast Creamery in 2012, and among their many exemplary cheeses, their first washed-rind variety, Dream Weaver, is our favorite. Past the fragrant notched rind is an bone-white paste studded with ragged eyes (holes) and supple texture. What's remarkable about Dream Weaver is how it expertly balances goat's milk tang with creamy sweetness and bready yeast flavors, making it both approachable and complex.

GOES BEST WITH: Sparkling brut rosato: What separates rosé, which most Americans are familiar with, from rosato, the Italian wine which also happens to be pink? In terms of how it's produced, nothing, but Italian grapes don't taste quite like French or Spanish or American grapes, so there are always subtle differences worth seeking out. And like rosé, one rosato can smell and taste markedly different from the next. Good brut rosato, such as the Sebastian Vino Spumante, will balance cantaloupe and tangerine sweetness with a dry finish and zippy acidity, with loads of cherries, oranges, and strawberries on the nose.

RESULTS

What a fun pairing sparkling rosato is with Dream Weaver! When these two come together, the tang from the goat's milk in the cheese drops way, way down as the yeast comes way, way up, fusing with the wine's fruity character and tasting exactly like **strawberry Pop-Tarts** smeared with **buttercream frosting**. If you grew up eating those sugary pastries, as we did, it's an immediate trip back in time to a more innocent era where nothing could surpass the joy of peeling back those flimsy foil packages and dropping the two frosted rectangles into the toaster.

QUICK BITE

Farmstead, Artisan, and Cooperative

The terms *farmstead*, *artisan*, and *cooperative* are thrown around a lot in the cheese vernacular, and the meaning of each helps tell the story of the cheeses they're connected to. The most romantic of the bunch, *farmstead*, refers to cheeses made on the same farm where the animals were milked, very much a singular affair. *Artisan* cheeses may not necessarily come from farms, but they're still very much handmade, with curds cut by hand and ladled into molds, using someone else's milk. *Cooperative* is more common in European cheesemaking, where several smaller farms pool their milk for a central cheesemaker and perhaps a separate affineur for the final aging. Although often abused and misused by corporations for marketing purposes, these terms reflect standards and traditions cheesemakers pride themselves upon, and represent products in which real humans played a part.

CHEESE		WINE	
Bucheron		CHÂTEAU DE ROQUEFORT **Corail Rosé**	
country of origin	*alternatives*		
France	Veigadarte	*country of origin*	*other suggestions*
family	Zingerman's Lincoln Log	France	Wilfrid Rousse Rosé de Saignée Chinon
Bloomy-rind	Capriole Farmstead Old Kentucky Tomme	*style* Still French rosé	Mas de Cadenet Côtes de Provence Sainte-Victoire Rosé
milk			
Goat			

ABOUT THE CHEESE: France's Loire Valley is widely accepted as the home of chèvre. Bucheron (from the French word for "log," *bûche*) was one of the first goat cheeses France exported to the United States, and its distinctive ivory log shape is a dead giveaway in any cheese case. Slicing into it reveals an interior like a Hostess snack cake: gooey cream where the cheese has started to break down under the rind, pasty white chèvre filling the center. The contrast between the salty cream and the lemony, pleasantly goaty chèvre is like getting two world-class cheeses in one, and that's before you even introduce a beverage to the mix.

GOES BEST WITH: Still French rosé: The fact that we have multiple styles of rosé in this book should tell you how highly we regard this elegantly fruity pink beverage as a companion for cheese. In the South of France, several exemplary still rosés emerge from Languedoc-Roussillon, Provence, and the Rhône, and you shouldn't have any trouble securing one from your local bottle shop. Depending on the dominant grape used and how much of the sugars are allowed to ferment, the rosé may be dry (Sangiovese, Syrah, Grenache) or sweet (merlot, white zinfandel), but most fall into an agreeable middle ground that goes hand in hand with cheese.

RESULTS

When Bucheron's involved, we go with dry still rosé, because the salt in the cheese trims back the wine's acidity without getting its more delicate flavors washed out by scrubbing bubbles. Then, the wine's fruity attributes are laid bare for the cheese to embrace. When we tested this pairing, we were amazed at the accurate representation of **li hing mui (salted plum) shave ice** the combo produced. Try it out with your French rosé of choice and see which fruit the Bucheron snares.

QUICK BITE

Saignée

Another less common way to produce rosé is called *saignée* (French for "to bleed"). Typically, freshly pressed red grapes will be left to macerate on its skins and seeds to deepen its color during fermentation and increase its complexity over a long period of time. With saignée, some of the juice is "bled off" early on, before it has a chance to turn a darker shade of crimson. Postfermentation, the wine tends to be brawnier than a rosé produced with the more traditional method, but still lighter and fruitier than a full-blown red. Try one side by side with a non-saignée bottle and see whether you can tell the difference.

Robiola

country of origin	alternatives
Italy	Cravanzina
family	Green Dirt Farm Ruby
Fresh or bloomy-rind	Boxcarr Rosie's Robiola
milk	
Cow, sheep, and/or goat	

PODERE RUGGERI CORSINI
Langhe Rosato

country of origin	other suggestions
Italy	Masseria Li Veli Salento Rosato
style	
Still rosato	Muri-Gries Lagrein Kretzer Rosato Sudtirol

ABOUT THE CHEESE: Robiola is somewhat of a catchall for the fresh or soft-ripened cheeses of Italy's Piedmont and Lombardy regions, which can include any ratio of cow's, goat's, or sheep's milk, though many believe the original recipe was entirely goat (and some, such as Robiola di Roccaverano, still require at least 50% goat's milk). Although all are delicious, we prefer the bloomy-rinded variety without goat's milk for this pairing: the rind imparts an earthy mushroom flavor to the custardy paste.

GOES BEST WITH: Still rosato. Deciding between a sparkling rosato (the Italian persuasion of sparkling rosé) and a still one comes down to simple dynamics. A still rosato tends to blend with cheese a little easier, bringing the two elements into a pleasant middle ground, whereas a sparkling rosato will make certain flavors pop and dwarf others. On the still side, we like the Podere Ruggeri Corsini Langhe Rosato, an orangish, medium-bodied wine that lures you in rich with aromas of strawberries, rose petals, and plums, but then wallops you with a bright, spicy acidity and melons on the finish.

RESULTS

Here's another beautiful example of "what grows together goes together," especially if you have a rosato from the Langhe in Piedmont. Both the cheese and the wine are in a similar place texturally, so they blend seamlessly into a sweet, creamy, fruity cloak draped over your palate. The fat-rich Robiola calms the acids and tannins in the rosato, allowing the previously restrained **melon** notes to burst through like happy beams of sunshine on a Montferrat hillside.

CHEESE	WINE

Patacabra

DOMAINE DE LA SÉNÉCHALERIE
Folle Blanche

country of origin	*alternatives*	*country of origin*	*other suggestions*
Spain	Leonardo	France	Domaine Pierre Luneau-Papin Gros Plant du Pays Nantais
family	Garrotxa		
Washed-rind	Haystack Mountain	*style*	
	Queso de Mano	Folle Blanche	Jean Aubron Folle Blanche
milk			
Goat			

ABOUT THE CHEESE: Julian Cidraque's Patacabra (Spanish for "goat's leg") is notable not just for its unusual squashed-brick shape, but for its capricious nature: seasonal humidity will impact its appearance, aroma, and even its flavor. Typically, though, you can expect a lemony zip laced through a sour cream tanginess and subtle barnyard funk. The cheese starts to take on a pronounced olive quality the longer it ages and its texture turns from fudgy to crumbly, but the underlying flavors remain to enchant.

GOES BEST WITH: Folle Blanche. Known primarily for its use in Armagnac and other brandies, the Folle Blanche grape (also known as Gros Plant or Picpoule or some variation of those spellings) has endured near decimation at the hands of aphids that ravaged French vineyards in the 1800s. It's bracingly acidic, which makes for a tart, zesty wine with oodles of lime and green apple character.

The fun in pairing a Folle Blanche wine with Patacabra comes not so much from what they taste like together, but what *happens* when they meet. The tangy cheese and bright wine collide headlong with a smack to the palate that wakes you right up. Immediately after that audacious opening move, the acids cancel each out and fizzle away, giving you a few moments to savor the wine's minerality and the Patacabra's milkier aspects. But just as you lower your guard, the wine rises again, bringing with it a wave of unripe berries to tickle your tongue one last time.

CHEESE		WINE	

Tilsiter

country of origin	*alternatives*
Prussia/Switzerland	Maasdam
family	Bierkase
Washed-rind	Widmer's Aged Brick
milk	
Cow	

WEINGUT MANTLERHOF
Grüner Veltliner

country of origin	*other suggestions*
Germany	Weingut Nigl Kremser Freiheit Grüner Veltliner
style	
Grüner Veltliner	Weingut Emmerich Knoll Loibner Grüner Veltliner

ABOUT THE CHEESE: Tilsiter is one of those cheeses that walks right up to the cliff of Too Much and stops just short of going over the edge. Its pungent aroma, potent saltiness, prickly funk, and piquant nuttiness ensure that it stands out on any cheese plate despite its plain appearance. That's the Tilsiter we enjoy best, but the cheese varies significantly from country to country or even within the same country. Some, such as the Swiss "green label" variety, are mild and more elastic, punched through with irregular holes and more closely resembling Havarti. Those are perfectly fine, but to make this pairing really take off, you'll want to ask your cheesemonger for a sharper Tilsiter from Austria or even the Swiss "red label," made from raw milk.

GOES BEST WITH: Grüner Veltliner. When you're in the mood for something with real zip to it, reach for a bottle of Grüner Veltliner. The "green wine of Veltlin," usually produced in Austria, injects pizzazz into even the fattiest foods with a dry lemon-lime sizzle that'll wake you right up. Once your palate adjusts to the acidity, you'll start to pick up delicate flavors that also appear in the fruity nose: honeysuckle, green apple, orange blossom, underripe peaches, and maybe a little pepper and pine on the finish. Serve straight from the fridge.

RESULTS

Pairing Grüner Veltliner with Tilsiter sets up a roller-coaster ride through waves of funk from the cheese and fruit from the wine, each cutting through in stages to balance and accentuate the other. The Tilsiter also has the laudable effect of sweetening the wine, so the citrus that hits your palate is closer to **oranges** and **tangerines** than it is to lemon and limes. Then, just when you think you've seen all this pairing has to offer, it finishes in a deeply savory place: **French onion soup** with **thyme**. It all comes together somehow, dropping you in the middle of an Alpine forest far from anything near the twenty-first century.

QUICK BITE

Raw Milk—What's the Deal?

The phrase *raw milk* means simply milk that has not been pasteurized (heated sufficiently to kill off the many microbes naturally present in it). Many cheesemakers prefer to work with raw milk, as it has much more depth of flavor than the pasteurized stuff, but in the United States, a 1949 rule states that any FDA-inspected dairy can only use raw milk to make cheese if said cheese is aged for at least 60 days. That makes it impossible to sell or even import the young raw milk cheeses Europeans enjoy with abandon. As frustrating as that is, there are pasteurized versions of several of these famous raw milk cheeses available to Americans, and many are quite delicious in their own right. Just don't take one with you to France and taste them side by side unless you strongly disagree with the notion that ignorance is bliss.

CHEESE		WINE	
VON TRAPP		DOMAINE LEON BOESCH	
Oma		**"Pierres Rouges" Sylvaner**	
country of origin	*alternatives*		
United States (Vermont)	Tulip Tree Foxglove	*country of origin*	*other suggestions*
	Cato Corner Farm Hooligan	France	M. Chapoutier Schieferkopf Sylvaner
family		*style*	Trimbach Sylvaner
Washed-rind	Durrus	Alsace Sylvaner	
milk			
Cow			

ABOUT THE CHEESE: Three generations of von Trapps (yes, *Sound of Music* fans, those von Trapps) have owned and cared for the land in northern Vermont upon which the von Trapp Farmstead sits and their Jersey cows roam, but cheesemaking only entered the picture in 2009. Sebastian von Trapp named his creamery's first cheese Oma after his grandmother Erika (*oma* is German for "grandma"), and it's a beauty. With a firm, puddinglike consistency at room temperature, an earthy rind, and big funky flavors of brine, bacon fat, and salted peanuts, Oma easily holds its own on any cheese plate. von Trapp has aligned closely with Jasper Hill Farm to age Oma in its massive man-made, dynamite-blasted, temperature-controlled caves alongside cheeses from such creamery giants as Cabot or smaller operations like Scholten Family Farm.

GOES BEST WITH: Alsace sylvaner. Once Germany's most-planted wine grape, the high-acid Sylvaner (or Silvaner) has dropped off in popularity over the past century, but you'll still find it claiming plenty of vineyard real estate in certain areas. It's often criticized for its neutral flavors, but the grape is capable of producing wines ranging from bone dry to full-bodied, with plenty of nuance in between. The Alsace region produces some of the most underappreciated and

food-friendly wines in the world (sylvaner is aces with Alsatian Munster, page 118), so it's no small wonder it's brilliant with many different cheeses.

Sometimes bracingly tart like a grapefruit, lime, and green apple ménage à trois, the raciest versions of Alsatian sylvaner act as the ideal foil for Oma's rich opulence. Here, the cheese drapes over the wine like a warm winter blanket, smoothing down the acidic sylvaner's sharper edges. Simultaneously, the wine softens the cheese's funkier characteristics, producing hearty flavors like **stew** or **risotto** with a splash of **sherry vinegar**. The tangy wine returns on the finish after the cheese has played its part, cleansing the palate for another round.

Caves

The use of "caves" in the production of cheese came about out of necessity. Before electricity revolutionized the dairy industry, cheese had to be stored and aged in man-made cellars or naturally occurring underground caverns, whose cooler temperatures and high humidity were nearly ideal for the development process and preventing the cheese from rotting or drying out. The cave environment itself has a hand in shaping a cheese's flavor, with naturally occurring yeasts, molds, and bacteria imparting their own character; Roquefort is a great example of a cheese whose distinctive flavor comes from the cave-cultivated blue mold. Despite the advent of refrigeration, many cheesemakers continue to age their products in these damp caverns, preferring the personality of cave-aged cheeses to those matured in sanitized and temperature-controlled rooms.

CHEESE		WINE	
Munster		OVUM **Off the Grid Riesling**	
country of origin	*alternatives*		
France	Limburger	*country of origin*	*other suggestions*
family	Herve	United States (Oregon)	Domaine Zind Hunbrecht Riesling
Washed-rind	Consider Bardwell Farm Dorset	*style*	Hugel Riesling
milk		Riesling	
Cow			

ABOUT THE CHEESE: Now here's a challenging one for you. Not to be confused with the inoffensive Americanized deli cheese usually spelled Muenster, Munster hails from eastern France's Alsace-Lorraine, where it's been made from the milk of cows grazing in the Vosges Mountains since the seventh century. Originally a monastic product used in the abbeys to supplant meat on days of fasting, it's now protected by AOC designation (see page 86). Get anywhere near a wheel of Munster and you'll know it: its potent eggy aroma permeates the space around it, thanks to an orange rind encrusted with pungent fungi and bacteria. No quarter is given once the soft, supple cheese hits your mouth, enveloping your palate with an assertive, barnyardlike funk and sour tickle that gradually melts into a creamy, bacony finish. Not for the timid!

GOES BEST WITH: Riesling. Riesling's having a moment, which we couldn't be happier about. Riesling grapes are renowned for their high acidity, fragrant honey blossom aromas, and big nectar flavors, which makes the wine they produce stellar companions for cheese. Said wines range from bone dry to syrupy sweet, but they can be delightfully complex, layering their sugars with notes of pineapple and lemon curd and a rounded, crisp finish. They're also great for aging, if you've got the patience.

It takes a wine with the weight and body of Riesling to stand toe to toe with Alsatian Munster, and the result is a monster celebration of the savory. Riesling's inherent sweetness spreads through the cheese, drawing out flavors of **peat** and **woodsmoke**, especially near the rind. Then we move into areas of **horseradish** and **cabbage gratin**, before the Riesling's sugars rise up at the end. It's hearty and meaty and soul-filling, like a rustic meal cooked over a campfire.

CHEESE		WINE	
SEQUATCHIE COVE		**HELIOTERRA**	
## Dancing Fern		## Melon de Bourgogne	
country of origin	*alternatives*	*country of origin*	*other suggestions*
United States (Tennessee)	Reblochon, Abbaye de Tamié	United States (Oregon)	Perennial Vintners Melon de Bourgogne
family		*style*	
Washed-rind		Melon de Bourgogne/ Muscadet	Perle Bleue Château de la Jousselinière Sur Lie
milk			
Cow			

ABOUT THE CHEESE: Luscious, unctuous French Reblo-
chon is unavailable in America due to US raw milk restrictions. Lucky for us, a cheese inspired by it, Dancing Fern, is
more than a suitable stand-in, but that's selling it short: it
really is something special. Here, the raw milk ages past 60
days (thus making it legal to consume in the States), and the
gooey result is a cheese with the aroma of a barn and flavors
of cultured butter and funky mushrooms just this side of
bitter. A complex, sophisticated delight and further evidence
that Southern cheese exists beyond the pimento variety.

GOES BEST WITH: Melon de Bourgogne/Muscadet. Melon
de Bourgogne is best known as the sole grape in French
Muscadet, but American versions (almost entirely from
the Pacific Northwest) exist under the grape's name, or just
"Melon." Whatever appears on your bottle, this is a very dry,
light-bodied white with fruity melon and orange blossom
aromatics that do not represent the actual flavor of the wine.
Instead, you get a big hit of acidity and gooseberry tartness
up front, bookended by bitter citrus pith, pine, caraway seed,
pepper, and casual salinity. Some are aged *sur lie* (see the
Quick Bite), and these are generally much richer and yeastier.

RESULTS

Dancing Fern is just the right cheese to take the edge off Melon de Bourgogne wines. The cheese is so buttery that the wine's acidity has no choice but to mellow out, so the wine's remaining flavors get to step up and play with the Dancing Fern. The bitter note in the cheese and the citrus pith in the wine find common ground, complementing each other neatly. Meanwhile, the wine's more savory angles adjoin with the funky **shiitake** overtones in the cheese, forming a creamy, **umami-rich stew** in your mouth. Total bosom buddies, these two.

QUICK BITE

Sur Lie

If you happen to find a bottle of wine from the Loire Valley labeled "sur lie," know that those aren't just two random French words slapped onto the label. *Sur lie* means "on the lees," which is to say the wine within was aged on the spent yeast cells after the wine achieved fermentation, rather than being separated from them as would normally be the case. Why bother spending time leaving the wine to sit on a bed of yeast husks? From this aging, the wine gains a fuller, creamier body, with added yeasty aromas and flavors. Not better or worse than a wine with the lees filtered out, just different.

CHEESE	WINE		
CASCADIA CREAMERY # Sawtooth	**L'ECOLE NO. 41** # Sémillon		
country of origin United States (Washington)	*alternatives* Meadow Creek Grayson	*country of origin* United States (Washington)	*other suggestions* Peter Lehmann Marga- ret Barossa Sémillon
family Washed-rind	Canal Junction Charloe Durrus	*style* Sémillon	Cheval Quancard Premieres Côtes de Bordeaux
milk Cow			

ABOUT THE CHEESE: Named for the huckleberry-rich fields in Washington State's Gifford Pinchot National Forest, Sawtooth is an accessible, beverage-friendly, organic, raw milk, washed-rind cheese that revels in subtlety. Although it is deceptively simple at first taste, letting the cheese sit on your tongue awhile reveals shades of beef broth, fresh cream, and honeycomb, the flavors a whisper rather than a shout. Sawtooth, like all of Cascadia Creamery's cheeses, is aged in one of the area's prevalent lava tubes, where it picks up a slight funky note and mild peatiness—again, both gentle enough that no one flavor dominates.

GOES BEST WITH: Sémillon. Thin of skin but rich in fla-vor, the Sémillon grape originated in France's Bordeaux region, where it claims more vineyard acreage than any other white grape. Sémillon wine may not have the renown of those juggernauts, but its complexity of flavors and aro-mas make it just as worthy of quaffing. Depending on the ripeness of the grape in the wine you're drinking, you may get more citrus and green apple, or white melon and pear. Sémillon has a lot going on aromatically, with apple, pine-apple, and honeydew on the nose, so it's a real treat for the senses. We've also seen a rise in Australian Sémillon, which tends to have more tropical fruit flavors, thanks to the warmer climate. Give it a chance!

When you layer in the Sawtooth with a sip of a Sémillon wine, beautiful things happen. First, the cheese mellows out any oakiness in the wine, and a sweet **brown sugar** note rises to take its place. The combo finishes with **bittersweet white raspberries** and a sweet, funky aftertaste that's simply not present when you drink the wine solo. One heck of a nice way to finish a salty meal.

QUICK BITE

Washed-Rind Cheeses

Peering into your local cheesemonger's case, you spy a burnished orange-pink cheese beckoning you for a sample. The monger proffers a slice, its rind tacky to the touch. And boy oh boy does it stink to high heaven. What you have there is a washed-rind cheese, named so because these cheeses are literally washed in a salted brine meant to encourage the growth of a bacteria strain known as *Brevibacterium linens* (*B. linens* for short). Beyond the appearance and aroma, *B. linens* and the other bacteria and yeasts that find a home in the briny surface affect how the cheese will break down beneath the rind and ripen; these cheeses can become quite oozy and even runny as they close in on room temperature. Most noticeably, washing a cheese's rind develops exquisite umami flavors of rendered bacon fat, beef broth, and stewed onions. Prime examples include Époisses (page 83), Munster (page 118), Red Hawk (page 186), and Tilsiter (page 114).

CHEESE		WINE	
Gabietou		DOMAINE DUPEUBLE PÈRE ET FILS **Beaujolais Blanc**	
country of origin	*alternatives*		
France	Vermont Shepherd	*country of origin*	*other suggestions*
	Verano	France	Jean-Paul Brun Terres
family	Carr Valley Cave-Aged		Dorées Beaujolais
Washed-rind	Marisa	*style*	Blanc
milk	Bamalou	Beaujolais Blanc	Domaine André Cologne
Cow and sheep			et Fils Baltha z'Arts
			Beaujolais Blanc

ABOUT THE CHEESE: A prime example of a transhumance cheese (see page 144), Gabietou hails from the French side of the Pyrenees, where the cows and ewes that produce its milk graze on high-elevation grasses in the summer. Different French *affineurs* take a crack at aging Gabietou the way they like best, which can mean rubbing the rind with salty brine to coax specific strains of bacteria to develop and ripen the cheese, or aging it on wooden planks to impart a unique flavor. Dense but supple, the cheese flaunts its buttery richness to great effect but works in a touch of sweetness from the sheep's milk that brightens up everything.

GOES BEST WITH: Beaujolais Blanc. Comprising a narrow swath of granite-laden countryside north of Lyon, Beaujolais produces some of France's best wine without any of the pretense or prestige heaped on the country's biggest names (your Burgundies and Bordeaux and what have you). Although Gamay wines are the predominant export of the region, Beaujolais Blanc uses Chardonnay grapes to mimic the attributes of crisp, dry ciders, meaning lots of Granny Smith and lots of acidity without an overwhelming tartness. These wines often give off an aroma of peach and apple skin, leading you seamlessly into every sip.

RESULTS

Bringing Gabietou into the mix cuts back on that acidity mightily, allowing the buttery side of the cheese to jostle its way to the front. What's left is luscious **cream**, a mild **fruity sweetness**, and a dash of **vanilla**. In other words, **cheese Danish**.

QUICK BITE

Affineurs

Affineurs (agers) have served as an instrumental component of the cheesemaking tradition in Europe for centuries. Sure, it's a science, but there's an art to it as well. In many prominent cheesemaking regions, such as the Jura in France, the cheesemaker will deliver young, "green" cheese to the affineur, who takes on the task of caring for and maturing the cheese up to the point it's ready to be sold and consumed. Affineurs don't simply stick the cheese on a shelf, then sit around and watch the cheese get old; their responsibilities include turning the cheese regularly to distribute the moisture within evenly, patting or rubbing the cheese to control the growth of mold on the rind, and if the cheese calls for it, washing the rind with a brine to promote bacterial growth to coax it toward perfection. Affineurs of note include Hervé Mons and Rodolphe Le Meunier in France, Luigi Guffanti in Italy, and Frederic Von Tricht of Belgium. The tradition has even spread to this side of the pond with consummate cheese refiners like Vermont's Jasper Hill Farm, who built their own cheese caves for their Cellars at Jasper Hill project to age their own cheeses and cheeses from nearby creameries.

CHEESE		WINE	
VERMONT CREAMERY ## St. Albans		**DOMAINE DE LA GRAND'COUR** ## Fleurie	
country of origin United States (Vermont)	*alternatives* Il Nocciola Saint-Marcellin	*country of origin* France *style*	*other suggestions* Division Gamay Noir "Cru" Georges Descombes
family Soft-ripened	Robiola 3-Milk	Gamay	Morgon
milk Cow			

ABOUT THE CHEESE: Named for the nearby cooperative that supplies all of its cow's milk, Vermont Creamery's St. Albans has spent the last few years generating buzz in the cheese world, and for good reason. It's similar in many respects to the French Saint-Marcellin, though its flavors eschew the mushroomy in favor of freshly churned butter, artichoke hearts, and fruit, specifically apple skin. Perhaps its most attractive trait is its silky, smooth texture that borders on milky once the cheese reaches room temperature. St. Albans comes in its own little ceramic crock so you can bake it for a fonduelike experience, but for the purposes of this pairing, we suggest eating it uncooked.

GOES BEST WITH: Gamay. Although a relative of pinot noir, with which it shares many characteristics, gamay stands apart with an airier (sometimes described as "frothy") body and a bouquet of floral and plum aromas that makes drinking a glass a treat for the ol' olfactory system. While often one of the fruitier light-bodied red wines, gamay can be gutsier than you might expect, brimming with tart cherries interspersed with strawberries and raspberries, and maybe a dash of earth.

RESULTS

A signature "comparable" pairing (see page 34), velvety smooth gamay aligns seamlessly with velvety smooth St. Albans. The cheese and wine perform a deft balancing act, each permitting the other's subtleties—both in flavor and in texture—to come through unaltered. The resulting vibe is all summertime and **strawberries and cream.**

CHEESE		WINE	
Schlossberger		DIVISION WINE CO. **"Un" Pinot Noir**	
country of origin	*alternatives*		
Switzerland	Gruyère	*country of origin*	*other suggestions*
family	Farm at Doe Run St. Malachi	United States (Oregon)	Johan Vineyards Estate
Alpine-style	Roth's Private Reserve	*style*	Stoller Family Estate
milk		Oregon pinot noir	Dundee Hills
Cow			Kelley Fox Ahurani
			Fossil & Fawn Pinot Noir

ABOUT THE CHEESE: Not many cheeses are named after a medieval castle, but Schlossberger holds that honor. It comes in "young" and "mature" versions, with the former bearing many similarities to Swiss Emmentaler and the latter resembling Gruyère. The mature version is aged 15 months in caves near the remains of Castle Schlossberg, which enhances the cheese with crunchy protein crystals, salty beef broth overtones, and a nutty butterscotch sweetness.

GOES BEST WITH: Oregon pinot noir. Entire books can and have been written about pinot noir, a wine so popular it's among the 10 most planted grape varietals in the world. A red wine on the lighter end of the spectrum in both color and alcohol, pinot noir nevertheless exhibits a superb depth of character and precise balance, though its flavor profile varies considerably from region to region. Pinot noirs from Oregon's Willamette Valley tend to taste earthy and almost imperceptibly tart, like cranberries, apple skin, and just-shy-of-ripe cherries.

An absolutely brilliant pairing with "smooth" written all over it. Pinot noir turns Schlossberger into **buttery caramel** without losing its savory beefiness, especially if you're starting with the aged version of the cheese. Schlossberger evens out the wine's tannins and brings up a bright **cherry** note inflected with **sweet caramelized onions**, for a sweet and savory magic trick so deftly executed you'll swear this cheese was created solely to eat with pinot noir.

QUICK BITE

Biodynamic Farming, or Manure in the Cow's Horn

Ask a hundred winemakers about biodynamic farming and you'll likely receive just two opinions: deep reverence or outright ridicule. Predating organic farming by a couple of decades, biodynamic farming treats soil, plants, animals, water, air, light, darkness, even the moon and stars as a single interconnected ecosystem. Holistic and homeopathic in nature, it flatly rejects the use of any chemical aid, relying instead on an astrological calendar and some rather unconventional methods of composting to ensure the health of the land and grapes. How unconventional? Well, one widely used method of fertilizing the soil on a biodynamic farm is to stuff cow's horns with manure, bury the horns, leave them undisturbed over winter, then dig them up in the spring, empty the horns, and scatter the contents over the vineyard. Adhering to biodynamic farming's protocols also means only watering grapes on "Leaf Days" and harvesting only on "Fruit Days" (don't do anything on "Flower Days," though—that's a time of rest).

How do you know your wine is biodynamic? Look for the "Demeter" certification stamped on the label. Just don't expect to pick up any traces of horn in the nose or on the finish; biodynamic wines are indistinguishable from nonbiodynamic ones. Pseudoscience or not, biodynamic farming is essentially the same as organic farming, and the respect these farmers have for the land, keeping the soil and whatever grows in it free of pollutants, is laudable.

CHEESE		WINE	
Parmigiano-Reggiano		ANGÉLIQUE LÉON **Chinon**	
country of origin	*alternatives*		
Italy	Grana Padano	*country of origin*	*other suggestions*
family	Sapore del Piave	France	Olga Raffault Chinon Les Picasses
Cooked and pressed		*style*	Leah Jørgensen Cellars Loiregon Cabernet Franc
milk		Cabernet franc	
Cow			

ABOUT THE CHEESE: Another contender, along with Stilton, for the "King of Cheeses" title, though in America one is unquestionably more popular than the other. It may or may not surprise you that Parmigiano-Reggiano and true Parmesan are the same cheese, and no, we're not talking about the green canisters filled with salty powder labeled "Parmesan" in the local supermarket. This is an ancient cheese, long revered the world over and written about since the era of the Roman Empire. After a year of aging, the monster 80-pound wheels are inspected for structural imperfections with a small metal mallet, then inspected again six months later (sometimes even x-rayed!) before sale. Parm is at once grassy and fruity like strawberries, mildly salty, with a toasted walnut character, all balanced by a savory brothlike umami note that makes this cheese so special.

GOES BEST WITH: Cabernet franc. One of the fathers of cabernet sauvignon along with sauvignon blanc, the Cabernet Franc grape thrives in the cooler climate of France's Loire Valley, where it has grown for centuries, but you can find it elsewhere in France, as well as in Italy, Chile, and the West Coast of the United States. A common thread running through cab franc wines is a peppery spiciness mingling among reflections of raspberries, grape must, and a refresh-

ing minerality. It's an assertive, acidic red with funky/fruity aromas, a big hit of tannins, and a hint of smoke lingering in the background.

Parmigiano-Reggiano works like magic on cabernet franc. The tannins and acid drop right out of the wine and let all that wonderful, juicy fruit blossom like wildflowers in springtime. Ripe **bing cherries**, **raspberries**, and **cherry cordials** come through brightest, followed by **caramelized walnuts** and **cocoa**. In other words, a treat for everyone's sweet tooth.

CHEESE		WINE	

Andazul

country of origin	alternatives
Spain	Cabrales
	Bleu du Bocage
family	Pure Luck Farm
Blue	Hopelessly Bleu
milk	
Goat	

DOMAINE SKOURAS
Saint George Aghiorghitiko

country of origin	other suggestions
Greece	Nasiakos Agiorgitiko
	Nemea
style	Katogi & Strofilia
Agiorgitiko	Mountain Fish Agiorgitiko

ABOUT THE CHEESE: Blue cheeses made from goat's milk are already a rare breed; to see one emerge from the Andalusia region of southern Spain is practically a miracle. Its creator, Ana Rosado, keeps her production operation small to maintain quality control over the cheese, using milk from the indigenous (and endangered) Payoya goats brought to her by local herders and brushing the wheels with olive oil. Andazul's fairly congenial as far as blues go, with a mild acidic bite appropriately balanced by good salt levels and a buttery finish.

GOES BEST WITH: Agiorgitiko. While its name may sound like something you'd wail unintelligibly after stepping barefoot on a LEGO block, Agiorgitiko (or more easily pronounced, "St. George") is a Greek red wine with a remarkably versatile exhibition of flavors, depending on the vineyard and vintage. Typical characteristics include a plum-and-raspberry fruitiness, aniseed spiciness, and low tannins, but we've tasted some with an herbaceous nose and flavors of green tea, cherries, and chocolate.

"Sweet and meaty" probably isn't how you'd describe something you're trying to convince someone else to eat, but stay with us here, it all works out in the end. After a bite of Andazul, a splash of Agiorgitiko draws out a steaklike note in the cheese, focusing it until it takes on the flavors of a nice **flank of goat**—one that probably ate a lot of **hazelnuts** in its time. The Andazul in turn brings out a fruity sweetness in the wine, full of **juicy ripe cherries**, a perfect accompaniment for roast goat. Hence, sweet and meaty. Hungry now?

CHEESE		WINE	

Pecorino Sardo

country of origin	*alternatives*
Italy	Fiore Sardo
family	Pecorino Toscano
Cooked and pressed	Stagionato
	Bellwether Farms
milk	San Andreas
Sheep	

PACINA
Toscana Sangiovese

country of origin	*other suggestions*
Italy	Felsina Berardenga
	Fontalloro Toscana
style	Montesecondo Rosso
Toscana red	

ABOUT THE CHEESE: Don't read "Pecorino" and move on without a thought—that "Sardo" up there, a reference to the Italian island of Sardinia, separates this cheese from the more prevalent Pecorino Romano (also, confusingly, made on Sardinia). Although they share some similarities texturally, they don't taste anything alike. While Pecorino Romano is intensely salty, Pecorino Sardo takes an earthier tack, with rustic inclinations of soil, moss, and hay that may trick you into thinking it's smoked (though some varieties do undergo some smoking). That particular combination of flavors make this a difficult cheese to pair with beverages, so tread carefully (or just let us do the work for you and keep reading!).

GOES BEST WITH: Toscana red. Despite flaunting one of Earth's most breathtakingly beautiful landscapes, Tuscany is rife with rock-, clay-, and sand-heavy soil lacking the density of nutrients required for many crops to flourish. But it's under those infertile conditions that the Sangiovese grape thrives and produces robust wines highly representative of their terroir. Earthy, tannic flavors abound, presaged by massive aromas of black cherry and leather—that "new car smell" in a glass.

RESULTS This is a thoroughly comparable matchup that finds common ground . . . in the ground, taking the earthy, damp qualities in both the cheese and the wine and blasting them into the stratosphere. Any fruitiness in the wine immediately exits stage left as one musty, savory note after another spreads across your palate. With each nibble of Pecorino Sardo and sip of wine, we picked up a new round of flavors: first **moss** and **soil**, then **terra-cotta** and **clay**, and finally **roasted garlic**. It's heavily evocative of the lee side of an old Italian farmhouse and there's nothing else in this book like it.

QUICK BITE

Sheep and Their Cheeses

Between sheep, goats, and cows, the three animals that fuel the vast majority of the world's cheese supply, sheep generate the smallest amount of milk, yet sheep were milked by humans before a cow's udder ever entered our hands. Here in the United States, sheep kept for dairy purposes are dwarfed by those kept for wool or meat, but dedicated cheesemakers are slowly making headway at upping our population. The most common dairy sheep is the East Friesian; others include the Basco-béarnaise, Manchega, Sarda, and Lacaune.

With nearly twice as much fat as cow's milk, sheep's milk seems tailor-made for cheesemaking, but sheep's short lactation cycle makes for low yields, and several cheeses exhibit a note of lanolin that manifests as a "wool sweater" flavor that can clash with certain beverages (trust us on that one). Sheep's milk's richness trumps all, however, and is fully apparent when you dive into the classic sheep cheeses, including Roquefort (page 147), Pecorino Sardo (page 133), Manchego (page 156), and Ossau-Iraty (page 143).

CHEESE	WINE
LA GRUTA DEL SOL	CHÂTEAU GAZIN
# Tres Leches	# Pomerol

country of origin	*alternatives*	*country of origin*	*other suggestions*
Spain	Carr Valley Gran Canaria	France	Clos Fourtet St-Émilion 1er Grand Cru Classé B
family	Hook's Triple Play Extra Innings	*style*	Château Joanin Becot Côtes de Bordeaux Castillon
Natural rind		Right Bank Bordeaux blend	
milk			
Cow, sheep, and goat			

ABOUT THE CHEESE: Point of clarity: there are actually two cheeses named "Tres Leches" coming out of Spain, one from Rio Deva Dairy and one from La Gruta del Sol (there may be others we're unaware of, but those are the biggies). The Rio Deva Tres Leches is a semisoft, bloomy-rind cheese with mild flavors of fresh cream, and while that's a fine cheese, the one from La Gruta del Sol is what you want to find for this pairing. Rubbed with olive oil at least three times during its six-plus months of aging, this Tres Leches glorifies the richest aspects of cow's, sheep's, and goat's milk and tastes like a concentrated blend of hard-boiled egg yolk, caramel, and crushed peanuts. A secret weapon for any cheese plate needing a kick in the pants.

GOES BEST WITH: Right Bank Bordeaux blend. With easy access to the sea, Bordeaux in southwest France played a crucial role in getting its wines to other countries in Europe and beyond, one massive reason wines from this fertile region have earned and maintained so much cachet for so long. Luscious red wines from Bordeaux's Right Bank (see the Quick Bite) rely heavily on Merlot grapes, with support from Cabernet Franc and Cabernet Sauvignon, so a random bottle plucked from this area will tend to be smooth and low in tannins, with subtle flickers of plum, tobacco, and vegetation on the nose, and black currant and cassis on the palate.

RESULTS

Pairing a Right Bank Bordeaux blend with Tres Leches sends you off in two totally different directions that somehow meet in a very complementary way at the end. Let's start with the wine. Instead of accentuating the sweet fruit, as usually happens with cheese and wine, Tres Leches pulls out green flavors of bitter **frisée** or **radicchio**. On the cheese side, the Bordeaux blend focuses all its attention on Tres Leches' uncanny **egg yolk** flavor. Hold on . . . frisée, egg yolk . . . yes, it's **salade lyonnaise**. All that's missing is a little bacon.

QUICK BITE

Left Bank vs. Right Bank

Let's start with a little geography. The city of Bordeaux sits near the convergence of two rivers flowing northwest, the Dordogne to the north and the Garonne to the south; the rivers feed into the Gironde Estuary, which dumps into the Atlantic. The land to the south of this estuary and the Garonne is known as the Left Bank, and the land to the north of the estuary and the Dordogne is the Right Bank (the land between the two rivers is called the Entre-Deux-Mers, but that's neither here nor there). Despite their proximity, the two banks have vastly different terroir. Whereas the Left Bank's soil is top-heavy with gravel and with nutrient-rich limestone buried deep, the Right Bank gets the limestone much closer to the surface, meaning grapes grow much more easily there. Cabernet Sauvignon is the Left Bank's dominant grape, and these wines are heavier on the tannins and better for aging. To the north, Merlot is *nombre un*, meaning Right Bank wines have less palate-drying tannins and are better consumed fresh, generally.

CHEESE		WINE	

RAM HALL FARM
Berkswell

CLOS LA COUTALE
Cahors

country of origin	*alternatives*	*country of origin*	*other suggestions*
England	Vermont Shepherd Verano	France	Château Haut-Monplaisir Prestige Cahors
family	Hidden Springs Ocooch Mountain	*style*	Domaine Cosse Maisonneuve Cahors Solis
Cooked and pressed		Cahors	
milk	Otterbein Acres Shepherd's Delight		
Sheep			

ABOUT THE CHEESE: Resembling nothing so much as a small, rusty UFO, Berkswell started out as the Fletcher family's loose interpretation of Caerphilly, another hard cheese, which they molded in kitchen colanders to produce its unforgettable shape. First impressions of Berkswell are bound to remind you of the lanolin-rich flavor of Pecorino Romano, without the intense saltiness that cheese is known for, though early-season wheels (when the sheep's diet turns from siloed corn to pasture grasses) will taste much fruitier, with notes of dried pineapple and strawberries over a cozy roux-like base. The cheese is still made today on Ram Hall Farm in the West Midlands, still molded in those ordinary kitchen colanders. Why switch them out for something fancier when they're perfectly suited to the task?

GOES BEST WITH: Cahors. The picturesque medieval French town of Cahors, surrounded by the River Lot and clay-heavy soils of southwestern France, is the home of the Malbec grape, whose juice is such a deep shade of purple that its wine is called "black." Cahors wines are typically in the 80 percent Malbec range, with Tannat or Merlot covering the rest. The difference between the bouquet of a Cahors wine and how it actually tastes is striking, all iron and blood and spice on the nose, followed by expansive cherry flavors cut by cherry pit bitterness that feels at once refined and rustic.

No question, the cherry essence that courses through Cahors's veins dominates this pairing. The Berkswell zeroes in on those fruity notes and their accompanying sugars while masking almost all of the wine's tannins, letting lightly sweetened cherries permeate everything that follows. **Cherry candy**, **cherry pie**, **cherry whipped cream**, it's all there, none of it so sweet as to burn out your palate, just sweet enough to conclude a meal on a high note.

CHEESE	WINE

UPLANDS DAIRY
Pleasant Ridge Reserve

country of origin	*alternative*
United States (Wisconsin)	Beaufort
	Comté
family	German ALEX
Alpine-style	Consider Bardwell Farm Rupert
milk	
Cow	

EDMUNDS ST. JOHN
Rocks and Gravel

country of origin	*other suggestions*
United States (California)	Tablas Creek Esprit de Tablas
style	Beckmen Cuvée Le Bec
California Rhône-style red blends	

ABOUT THE CHEESE: The only cheese to have won Best of Show three times at the American Cheese Society's annual competition, Pleasant Ridge Reserve comes with bovine-size expectations; thankfully, it lives up to all of them. Uplands Dairy follows the traditions of Alpine cheesemakers (see the transhumance Quick Bite on page 144) and only uses its cows' milk from mid-May to mid-October for this cheese (and if the pasture conditions aren't ideal, Uplands just sells off the milk). The dense cheese embodies a cashewlike nuttiness in a very Gruyère sort of way, with a salted caramel backbone that melts in your mouth. Uplands Dairy also makes a toothsome "extra-aged" version that amps up the crunchy tyrosine crystals and rich caramel flavor to decadent levels.

GOES BEST WITH: California Rhône-style red blends. France may have Côtes du Rhône appellation control over the blended wines coming from the prized namesake region, but that doesn't mean those same grape varietals can't make dynamite wine elsewhere. Take California, for instance. What the red blends from the Golden State's Central Coast lack in earthiness they make up for in robust, jammy raspberries, bing cherries, plums, and stone fruit. Most of these blends use Syrah, Grenache, Cinsault, and Mourvèdre grapes in

varying ratios, so no two will be quite the same, but whether you're picking up undertones of espresso or dark spices, that fruit-forward character will be unmissable.

Grab your favorite California Rhône-style red blend and try it with a nibble of Pleasant Ridge Reserve when you're in the mood for dessert: the flavors that bloom when these two meet conjure up images of a big bowl of **cherry pie à la mode** rimmed with **rich, buttery pastry dough**. The cheese takes those big fruity flavors in the wine and blows them up to royal proportions.

CHEESE		WINE	
Ossau-Iraty		DOMAINE DE DURBAN **Muscat de Beaumes de Venise**	
country of origin France	*alternatives* Le Berger Basque		
family Pressed and uncooked Pyrenees-style	Grafton Village Cheese Bear Hill Landmark Anabasque	*country of origin* France	*other suggestions* Domaine des Bernardins Muscat Beaumes de Venise
milk Sheep		*style* Muscat Blanc	Domaine de Fenouillet Muscat de Beaumes de Venise

ABOUT THE CHEESE: Ossau-Iraty is one of the world's oldest cheeses and one of the easiest to pair despite its sheep's milk provenance (cheese from ewe's milk tends to embody wooly lanolin notes). This firm, rich, ivory delight originated in the western Pyrenees between the Basque and Bearn regions of France and Spain, where shepherds allowed their sheep to graze in both high and low elevations in a process known as transhumance (see Quick Bite). You can tell if your Ossau-Iraty comes from a farmstead or a traditional dairy by the sheep stamp in the rind: a head-on ewe's head means it's the farm variety, and a side view means it's dairy-made. Expect earthy flavors of salty churned butter, cracked wheat, and roasted nuts, with hints of herbs and an underlying caramel sweetness that makes even cheese newbies fall in love.

GOES BEST WITH: Muscat Blanc. The term "Muscat" encompasses not a single grape, but more than 200 varietals ranging in color and style, used to produce lush, balanced, generally sweeter wines. It's also one of the oldest grapes around; even the ancient Greeks were drinking Muscat Blanc wines. Of the myriad Muscat clones, Muscat Blanc and the wines made from it are particularly agreeable to cheese with their intoxicating floral aromas and strong honey presence on the palate.

The Muscat we found that pairs best with Ossau-Iraty is made from the small, aromatic Blanc à Petits Grains grapes, which produces a wine with a valley-in-springtime nose of violets and rose petals. Those rose petals carry over into the flavor, joining ripe peaches and apricot preserves. Add the Ossau-Iraty and the wine's cloying sugars retreat, forming a perfect counterbalance between sweet and salty. With the sweetness reduced, the wine's fruitiness steps forward, pairing with the richness of the cheese like **peaches and cream** or **fresh yogurt**.

QUICK BITE

Transhumance

Mountain cheeses, such as Comté and Ossau-Iraty, often find their provenance in the grand tradition of transhumance (Latin for "over ground"), which involves migrating livestock to higher elevations in the summer and lower elevations in the winter. This practice allows the grasses on the lower pastures to grow in the summer, leaving an ample supply of hay for the animals when they return in the winter. There's a certain romance to cheese made in this manner, often inside small stone huts, where the milk is poured into grand copper kettles, heated over wood fires, and eventually formed into massive wheels to bring down the mountain to market. These cheeses tend to have deeper, more vivid flavors due to the fresh vegetation consumed by the cows on the higher pastures. So, if you're starting to pick out the taste of herbs or flowers in that Ossau-Iraty, chances are good transhumance played a part.

CHEESE	WINE

Roquefort

country of origin	alternatives
France	Hidden Springs
	Bohemian Blue
Family	Old Chatham
Blue	Ewe's Blue
milk	Hook's Little Boy Blue
Sheep	

CAMIN LARREDYA
Jurançon au Capceu

country of origin	other suggestions
France	Château les Astous
	Jurançon
style	Domaine Bellegarde
Jurançon Moelleux	Cuvée Tradition
	Jurançon Moelleux

ABOUT THE CHEESE: For six months of the year, in row upon row in the caves beneath Roquefort-sur-Soulzon at the base of the Combalou cliffs, ripening wheels of needle-lanced sheep's milk blue cheese fill the damp chilly air with an intoxicating pungency unlike any other on this planet. This quaint village in southern France is the only location Roquefort, dubbed the "king of cheeses" by philosopher Denis Diderot, can be made, per AOC designation (see page 86), though King Charles VI gave the town soul ownership of the cheese's name and methods way back in 1411! Roquefort receives its characteristic blue-green veins and funky flavors through the introduction of *Penicillium roqueforti;* two of the cheese's seven producers even cultivate it using the traditional method of leaving rye bread in the caves for the mold to consume. The finished cheese (in packaging marked by the telltale red ewe) doesn't assault the palate like some blues, but you can expect a balance between buttery richness, salty tang, and peppery sweetness.

GOES BEST WITH: Jurançon Moelleux. The Jurançon wine region in the foothills of the Pyrenees of southwestern France produces both dry (*sec*) and sweet (*moelleux*) wines, and when you've got a nice hunk of Roquefort, reach for the moelleux. Made principally from the Petit Manseng grape, which is harvested late in the season to allow the grape to

RESULTS

dehydrate and concentrate its sugars, Jurançon can catch you off guard if you're not anticipating an intensely sweet and fruity experience. Pour a glass, give it a swirl, and breathe in deeply for a one-way ticket to a summer orchard redolent of juicy peaches and honeysuckle. Each syrup-sweet sip delivers massive flavors of mango, honey, and apricot preserves but somehow finishes dry, allowing you to take another sip with your palate intact.

You need a rich, complex, palate-coating cheese like Roquefort to have any chance at all of standing up to a wine so assertive. The beauty of this pairing is that Roquefort diminishes the Jurançon's sweetness, meaning you can enjoy the wine anytime the mood strikes you and not just as an aperitif or with dessert. With a nugget of cheese and a thimbleful of wine, the holy matrimony of Roquefort and Jurançon takes on the complex, nutty, rich, yet undeniably fruity flavors of a **pear, walnut, and blue cheese salad**. Both components are stellar alone, but together they're simply stunning.

CHEESE		WINE	
POINT REYES		**TIO DIEGO**	
# Bay Blue		# Amontillado Sherry	
country of origin	*alternatives*	*country of origin*	*other suggestions*
United States	Great Hill Blue	Spain	González Byass Cuatro Palmas Amontillado
(California)	Northern Lights Blue	*style*	Lustau Very Rare Amontillado
family	La Peral Blue	Amontillado	
Blue			
milk			
Cow			

ABOUT THE CHEESE: Long before making cheese their focus, generations of the Giacomini family herded Holsteins and sold milk to the local creamery from their farm near Tomales Bay in Northern California. After reducing the size of the dairy and founding the Point Reyes Farmstead Cheese Company in 2000, owners Bob and Dean Giacomini and their four daughters crafted a portfolio of award-winning cheeses, chief among them the accessible but undoubtedly complex Bay Blue. Although milder and much sweeter than Stilton, it mirrors that legendary cheese's texture of fudge with a gritty galaxy of blue mold mottled throughout the tender paste. It reminds us a little of vanilla ice cream, specifically the ribbon of melting cream clinging to the edge of the bowl when you're halfway through it. Even professed blue haters find it agreeable!

GOES BEST WITH: Amontillado. In the famous Edgar Allen Poe story, Montresor effortlessly lures his nemesis Fortunato to his doom at the promise of a rare vintage of Amontillado, which says something about the desirability of this long-aged sherry. Amontillado starts out as fino, which is a dry, pale sherry wine made from the Palomino grape aged under a layer of flor yeast that protects it from exposure to air. The wine is then aged several more years in porous oak barrels that allow it to oxidize slowly. As the color deepens, the sherry begins to pick up aromas of nuts, fermented figs, leather, burnt sugar, and a near-indescribable ethereal quality. The stark dry finished wine crackles with zesty flavors of salted cherries, mint, and star anise. It's every bit as good as its reputation, so partake whenever you have the opportunity. Just be cautious around any friends inviting you down into dark catacombs to fetch a bottle.

The beauty of Bay Blue with Amontillado is that the cheese tames the wine's alcohol, stripping it back to lay bare its motley umami flavors that straddle the line between sweet and salty. **Bitter almonds, dark chocolate**, and **savory bread pudding** came through strongest for us, but each trip to the well revealed some new and exciting result that no other cheese and beverage combination could reproduce, so it's worth exploring with whatever Amontillado you can find in your local bottle shop.

QUICK BITE

Solera

Drinking most wine is largely an appreciation of vintage. One year, the weather may be warm and sunny, producing healthy grapes and subsequently stellar wine. Another year may lambast the vineyard with rain and chillier temperatures, resulting in sickly grapes and anemic wine. Some wines, though, such as sherry, avoid the vintage problem altogether through the process of *solera* (Spanish for "on the ground"), which ensures a consistent product year after year after year.

Imagine a stack of barrels three rows high. In Year One, fresh wine is added to the bottom row. In Year Two, the new fresh wine is added to the middle row and some is blended with the year-old wine in the bottom row. In Year Three, the fresh(est) wine is added to the top row and blended with the middle row, and the middle row is blended with the bottom row. Every year, some of the wine in the bottom row is drawn off and bottled, making room in the cask to add more wine from the row above; the middle row can then receive wine from the top row, and the top row can receive some of the current year's fresh wine.

The result is a deeply complex beverage made up of wines from several different vintages, which helps smooth out any one year's defects. The oxidation over such a long period develops flavors unique to the winery, treasured by ardent devotees. Although laborious and time-consuming, solera aging has spread to other alcoholic beverages, including rum, whiskey, and especially sour beers.

CHEESE		WINE	

Tomme de Savoie

WARRE'S
Otima 10 Year Port

country of origin	*alternatives*
France	Tomme Crayeuse
family	Saint-Nectaire
Tomme	
milk	
Cow	

country of origin	*other suggestions*
Portugal	Taylor Fladgate 10 Year Old Tawny Porto
style	Burmester 10 Tawny Porto
10-year tawny port	

ABOUT THE CHEESE: Even cursory research into Tomme de Savoie will reveal that most of it's produced with the skimmed milk left over from making butter, but don't worry about it tasting like a "lite" cheese; there's plenty of flavor and body here and you'd never know it was lower in fat if we didn't tell you. At first, Tomme de Savoie comes across earthy, with a fragrant rind not unlike a damp cellar. It quickly picks up a bit of tang and big walnut and nut butter flavors, balanced between sweet and salty. You may detect a little grassiness as well if it's from a younger wheel.

GOES BEST WITH: 10-year tawny port. What separates port from tawny port? Both are traditionally sweet, fortified wines (see the Quick Bite), but a lot more work goes into getting a tawny port from vine to bottle. It starts with blending older wines from Portugal's Duoro Valley and adding brandy to achieve a specific balance and sweetness. The new blend is then placed in oak barrels to age for several years, a process that oxidizes the wine and turns it from red to a ruddy . . . dare we say . . . *tawny* color. They typically come in 10-, 20-, 30-, and 40-year iterations (which indicates the average vintage of the wines comprising the tawny port), and the 10-year variety in particular goes swimmingly with cheese. On the nose, they give off a lot of oak from the barrel and a hint of Angostura bitters, but once it hits your mouth, it's all hazelnuts, figs, almond skin, and cola. Take it in quick sips; a mouthful will not only destroy your palate, it will ruin whatever cheese you throw on top of it!

RESULTS

Attention, nut lovers: this is your pairing! You've got Tomme de Savoie, heavy on the walnut, and then there's tawny port, heavy on the hazelnut and almonds. What do they taste like together? **Nuts on top of nuts of top of nuts**, with **cherry sweetness** flowing between the nutty layers. Sort of like a **peanut butter and jelly sandwich minus the bread**. The sweet wine also enhances the richness of the Tomme de Savoie and bolsters the cheese's funkier notes you might not have noticed otherwise. Truly a symbiotic relationship!

QUICK BITE

Fortified Wine

A wine that's been "fortified" means a distilled spirit—usually a neutral brandy—has been added to it. The resulting wine boasts a much higher alcohol content, but does not necessarily have to be sweet; it just depends on when the spirit was introduced to the mix. If the spirit is added while the wine is still fermenting, then the alcohol boost will kill off the yeast before it has a chance to convert all the available sugars, leaving you with a sweeter wine. Adding spirits *after* the wine has finished fermenting means the sugars have already fermented out, so the finished wine will be dry. Although originally wine was fortified to prevent it from degrading into vinegar on long sea voyages, it's now considered the perfect conclusion to a meal, whether dry like sherry or Marsala, or sweet like Madeira or port.

CHEESE WITH CIDER

CHEESE		CIDER	

CAPRIOLE
Wabash Cannonball

WOODCHUCK HARD CIDER
Amber

country of origin	*alternatives*	*country of origin*	*other suggestions*
United States (Indiana)	Valençay	United States (Vermont)	Crispin Original
family	Cypress Grove Humboldt Fog		Angry Orchard Crisp Apple
Mold-ripened	Veigadarte	*style*	
milk		American sweet	
Goat			

ABOUT THE CHEESE: Cribbing its name from the famous folk song about a legendary steam train that cut through Middle America around the turn of the century, Wabash Cannonball makes an unforgettable impression upon first sight as a wrinkled, ash-dusted, lopsided sphere resembling a little stone brain. The thick, creamy paste beneath that undulating surface is rife with citrusy goat's milk tang, offset by the sweet and earthy rind. With a shelf life of only about seven weeks, the cheese will change dramatically as it moves across that range, starting out white, smooth, and acidic and becoming grayer, crumbly, and mustier toward the end.

GOES BEST WITH: American sweet cider. We're starting out with the most widely available cider in the United States, the cider you can find in just about any grocery store no matter where you live: the sweet cider. Almost exclusively the territory of international beverage conglomerates, these mass-market ciders are designed to be as unchallenging and easily quaffed as possible by as many people as possible. Almost uniformly they give off apple Jolly Rancher aromas and taste somewhere between straight juice and grape soda, so they're best consumed very cold.

RESULTS

That is not to say that American sweet ciders don't have their place in the realm of beverage pairing, because the very goat-forward Wabash Cannonball is a cheese crying out for a sweet counterpart, a role these ciders fill most ably. While the cider tamps down the distinctive goatiness in the Wabash Cannonball and the funkier side of the rind, the thick, salty cheese really bites back on the cider's cloying sugars, taking both to a far more moderate place. That middle ground is a pleasant blend of **fondue** and **sweet cream**, one side's extremes balanced by the other's.

QUICK
BITE

The American Cider Resurgence(s)

Americans' love for liquor and beer, coupled with the fact that for more than a century cider in this country was made exclusively on farmsteads, all but extinguished any chances for the apple-centric beverage to gain a foothold in America. Technological advances and renewed interest in cider on both a local and national scale sent sales soaring in the early 1990s before crashing hard in the latter half of the decade. Most people had counted American cider out for good by that point, but the 2010s have flipped the script, with hard cider production in the US more than tripling from 2011 to 2013 and sales jumping a whopping 75 percent from 2013 to 2014 alone. Similarly eye-popping year-over-year gains have continued since, with corporate-owned brands' share of that wealth actually dropping in the past couple of years as regional brands' growth has risen. That's damn good news for cider drinkers: it means more quality cider more widely accessible to more parts of the country.

Manchego

country of origin	alternatives
Spain	Idiazábal
	Roncal
family	Zamorano
Uncooked and pressed	
milk	
Sheep	

BLACKBIRD CIDER WORKS
Premium Draft

country of origin	other suggestions
United States (New York)	Nomad Semi-Sweet
	Carlton Cyderworks Citizen
style	
American semisweet	

ABOUT THE CHEESE: Central Spain's windmill-dotted La Mancha plateau, immortalized in *Don Quixote*, seems an unlikely home for the country's most popular cheese, but tell that to the legion of Manchega sheep roaming its expansive plains. Aged Manchego represents its terroir to a T: dry, pale as a sun-bleached hillside, and thanks to a strong lanolin throughline, explicitly sheepy. As it ages, the cheese's nuttiness and meatiness increase, resting comfortably alongside its buttery constitution without going over the top.

GOES BEST WITH: American semisweet cider. Technically, a cider labeled "semisweet" contains up to 4 percent residual sugars, information that means very little to anyone until they actually take a drink. Nestled between full-on sweet and semidry, semisweet isn't shy about letting those sugars flaunt their stuff, which has the side effect of making the cider taste more like the amber supermarket apple juice we grew up with or even white grape juice, which is often associated with apple flavor.

RESULTS

Aged Manchego's salty dryness lends itself perfectly to a sweeter beverage. Once a splash of semisweet cider hits the cheese, it takes on the texture and flavor of **apple fruit leather** and **piecrust**, but the cider's sweetness doesn't overpower the milder Manchego. Instead, the cheese's salinity colors the fruitiness of the cider a shade of **salted plum** (our shave ice flavor of choice, by the way).

QUICK BITE

Johnny Appleseed

Few tales of American lore carry the altruistic warmth and wholesomeness of good ol' Johnny Appleseed walking across the country and scattering seeds randomly wherever his bare feet trod, leaving orchards of juicy fruit in his wake. Fact is, the real Appleseed, John Chapman, was a savvy businessman, capitalizing on a law allowing him to claim donation land upon which at least 50 apple trees were planted, then selling the fertile properties to settlers at a premium. And the apples he planted? Bitter and brutally tart, not for eating out of hand but ideal for fermenting into lucrative cider. Despite his distaste for footwear, he died a wealthy man and shaped the apple landscape in the United States forever.

CHEESE		CIDER	
Garrotxa		CIDER RIOT! **Everyday**	
country of origin	*alternatives*	*country of origin*	*other suggestions*
Spain	Twig Farm Goat Tomme	United States (Oregon)	ÆppelTreow Appely Doux
family	Crü di Capra	*style*	
Pyrenees-style	Goldin Artisan Tomme de Sawtell	American semidry	Meriwether Foothills Semi-Dry
milk			E.Z. Orchards Cidre Semi Dry
Goat			

ABOUT THE CHEESE: Were it not for the demise of Spain's Franco regime in the mid-1970s and the subsequent rise of small-production artisan cheese by Catalonia's self-described "neorural" urban hippies, we might never have had the opportunity to taste the wonderful Garrotxa today. The high humidity of the Pyrenees foothills is a breeding ground for *Penicillium* mold, which grows on Garrotxa's rind and subdues its acidity, producing a clean, mild, moderately tangy cheese with a truly lovely goat's milk–forward flavor and a texture that's alternately creamy and flaky. Just 10 families make it today, and only about a fifth of that production is exported, so it's worth snapping up a wedge when you find it.

GOES BEST WITH: American semidry cider. The difference between an American semidry cider and one produced in, say, England's West Country, can depend on the individual cidery, but generally US-produced ciders dial back on the bitter tannins the Brits so love, without letting the sugars get too out of hand. The best American versions offer a subtle range of flavors that require some concentration to appreciate, rather than bludgeoning you over the head with aromatics. Portland, Oregon's Cider Riot! makes a superb sparkling version with whispers of pineapple and tropical fruits, and just a pinch of sweetness. You'll often find semidry ciders labeled as "semisweet," but for the most part they're interchangeable.

RESULTS

The great thing about pairing American semidry cider with Spanish Garrotxa is how they twist each other into something new and fun. The cider brings out a huge coconut note in the cheese and raises the saltiness just a touch, and the cheese draws out tons of fruit and sweetness from the cider. Together, it's more than a little like **a bowl of Froot Loops with a splash of fresh coconut milk.**

QUICK BITE

Cider Apples

Any apple can be used to make cider, but a cider wrought entirely from sweeter varieties, such as Gala or Golden Delicious, will be a very humdrum cider indeed. The best ciders employ apples you'd never eat straight from the tree, though occasionally you'll find those familiar dessert varieties augmenting a blend of more multidimensional cultivars with such fun names as Foxwhelp, Tom Putt, and Harry Masters' Jersey.

Cider apples are divided into one four categories in a rubric devised by the Long Ashton Research Station outside Bristol in England, based on the apple's level of acidity and tannins:

- Bittersharp—High tannins, high acidity.
  Examples: Kingston Black, Porter's Perfection

- Bittersweet—High tannins, low acidity.
  Examples: Tremlett's Bitter, Brown Snout

- Sharp—Low tannins, high acidity.
  Examples: Wickson, Bramley's Seedling

- Sweet—Low tannins, low acidity.
  Examples: Sweet Alford, Fuji.

We can thank the Long Ashton Research Station and groundbreaking pomologists, such as Liz Copas, for studying and cataloging every facet of cider apples for cidermakers' benefit, and even creating brand-new varieties!

CHEESE		CIDER	

Vacherin Fribourgeois

VIRTUE CIDER
Michigan Brut

country of origin	*alternatives*		
Switzerland	Raclette Le Corbier	*country of origin*	*other suggestions*
	Appenzeller	United States	Foggy Ridge First Fruit
family	Spring Brook Farm	(Michigan)	Boulevard City Market
Washed-rind	Tarentaise		Dry Cider
		style	Hudson Valley
milk		American Dry	Farmhouse Cider God
Cow			Speed the Plough

ABOUT THE CHEESE: In western Switzerland's canton of Fribourg, home of Gruyère cheese, livestock herders follow the process of transhumance (see page 144) by migrating their cows from high Alpine pastures in the summer to low-level areas in the fall. Varying the cows' diet between mountain grasses and flowers one season and summer hay in the next, as well as only using raw milk and aging it in a damp cellar, leaves the resulting cheese, Vacherin Fribourgeois, positively tingling with flavor. This is a cheese with real bite, an acidic tang married to a funky, slightly sour flavor limned with herbaceous highlights, all in a smooth, creamy package. It comes in six variations of increasing intensity and goes great in fondue, but eat it straight off the wheel to get the full experience.

GOES BEST WITH: American dry cider. Nobody's going to top Great Britain in a dryness contest when it comes to cider; its definition of *dry* is simply on another level. In the United States, what some cideries call dry, a UK cidery may call off-dry, semidry, or even semisweet. That's not to say some cidermakers don't strip every last trace of sugar from their dry cider, because some have definitely left us smacking our lips. Dry cider should have very little residual sweetness and big, dusty tannins, which doesn't have to mean limited apple character. In fact, the apple should come through strongest

on the nose as fragrant spring apple blossoms, and on the palate in the form of tart green apple skin, with just a glimmer of sweetness peeking out from behind it.

An onslaught of dry cider's bitter tannins calls for a cheese that can really throw its weight around, and Vacherin Fribourgeois is more than up to the task. The cheese collides with the tannins and breaks them up, reducing the overall bitterness and letting the apple come up a little higher in the mix. Once Vacherin's twin pillars of creaminess and funkiness get their hooks into the cider's apple core (no pun intended), the flavors don't so much change as they escalate, just with an apple slant to them. Let's do the math: Creamy + Funky + Apple = **apple Greek yogurt**.

Clothbound Cheddar

ASPALL
Imperial English Cider

country of origin	*alternatives*
Debatable	Hafod
family	Quickes
Cheddar (milled-curd)	Bleu Mont
milk	Face Rock
Cow	

country of origin	*other suggestions*
England	Oldfields Worcestershire Medium Dry
style	Burrow Hill Somerset Medium Dry Cider
English semidry	Fowey Valley Castledore

ABOUT THE CHEESE: While Cryovac-sealed or wax-coated Cheddars are almost totally safe from the elements and the shrinking powers of evaporation, not to mention friendly to methods of mass production, clothbound Cheddars revel in outside influences—and are all the more flavorful for them. After the curds shed their whey, they're shaped into a wheel and left to age covered in fat (usually lard or butter) and a cotton wrap. The resulting drier, more concentrated cheese presents a wallop of tang interlaced with a grape-like fruitiness, wild onions, horseradish, and an earthy cellar aroma. Such varieties as the Isle of Mull Cheddar can harbor an almost briney quality to them, evoking the salt spray of the sea permeating the island's air. Expect to pay more for these cheeses, given how much more difficult they are to produce, but trust us: they're worth every penny.

GOES BEST WITH: English semidry cider. Once a regularly quaffed beverage here in the New World, American cider's been playing a serious game of catch up since its decline in the nineteenth century, and most of the supermarket is so artificial and sweet that just looking at the bottles can give you cavities (though these ciders *can* work well with cheese). Meanwhile, across the Atlantic, Brits have enjoyed the pleasures of dry, crisp, tannin-rich ciders for centuries, and they continue to drink about half of all the cider on the planet.

(Fun fact: All British citizens are entitled to produce up to 7,000 liters of cider every year tax-free!) Lucky for us Yanks, bottle shops are now regularly carrying these imported wonders, so we're quickly discovering what we've been missing. Ciders, especially farmhouse English ones, can be so dry they're like the most tannic white wines, so when you've got a clothbound Cheddar you'll want a cider that's *mostly* dry but still retains a fraction of sweetness.

This is one of those pairings that made us put down our glass and nod knowingly at each other as the cheese and cider merged into something greater than the sum of its (admittedly great) parts. Flavors of **rich plum pudding**, **stewed dark fruits**, and **mincemeat pie in a buttery crust** bloom magnificently, tempering the Cheddar's savory notes and deepening the cider's innate qualities as a dessert. *Delicious* doesn't begin to describe it . . . but it's a start.

QUICK BITE

Cheddaring

Originating in southwest England's Somerset county, cheddaring is what makes Cheddar . . . Cheddar. Here's how it works: Once the curd is formed and starts to separate from the whey, it's piled together on either side of a long trough and cut into large slabs that get stacked on top of each other. The slabs are repeatedly flipped and stacked, forcing more whey out and compressing the curds, which develops Cheddar's dense body and texture. When enough moisture is sufficiently forced out of the curds, the compressed blocks are milled into chunks about the size of your thumb, salted, and pressed into molds, ready for aging.

CHEESE		CIDER	

Gubbeen

country of origin
Ireland

family
Washed-rind

milk
Cow

alternatives
Meadow Creek
Grayson

Nicasio Square

Durrus

WORLEY'S CIDER
Mendip Hills

country of origin
England

style
English dry

other suggestions
Oliver's Traditional
Cider

Cornish Orchards Dry
Wharf Cider

ABOUT THE CHEESE: On an emerald green finger of land jutting into the Atlantic out of southwest Ireland, the sixth generation of the Ferguson family quietly makes some of the finest cheeses you'll find anywhere. Their herds of Jersey, Friesian, Kerry, and Simmental cows roam the pastures of the Cork County farm and produce the milk that eventually ends up as Gubbeen, a washed-rind cheese with flavors of rich butter, sweet cream, and cremini mushrooms. Don't toss the rind: it's covered in a one-of-a-kind pink-orange microflora unique to the area, and it brings an extra twist of funk and forest floor to an already distinct cheese.

GOES BEST WITH: English dry cider. Most proper cider from England is several notches drier than anyone else's, but the truly dry stuff is a showcase for tongue-twisting tannins and bittersweet or bittersharp apples. It's austere, yet anything but simple. Celtic Britons were making cider at least by the time of the Roman invasion, if not before, notably in Herefordshire and Somerset County, where cider apples grow in abundance. Large, industrialized producers, such as Bulmers, have dominated the modern market with substandard ciders, but independent farmhouse cider-makers are still putting out stellar examples that layer bitterness with tartness without losing the character of the apples.

RESULTS

A good dry English cider and a hunk of Gubbeen have the power to transport you to an old cabin in the woods where a **stew of beef and onions** simmers in a cauldron over a smoky fire. A little **peat** works its way into the mix, especially when you get a big piece of Gubbeen's unique rind, but the cider comes right behind it to scrape your tongue clean for another bite. This is rainy day comfort food at its best.

CHEESE		CIDER	
DE ZEEKRAAL		WANDERING AENGUS	
# Terschelling		# Wickson	
country of origin	*alternatives*	*country of origin*	*other suggestions*
Holland	Cypress Grove	United States (Oregon)	Uncle John's Baldwin
	Lamb Chopper		Embark Craft
family	Ewephoria	*style*	Ciderworks Crab Series
Gouda		Single-varietal	Distillery Lane
milk			Kingston Black
Sheep			

ABOUT THE CHEESE: Hailing from the island of the same name in the Wadden Sea north of Amsterdam, Terschelling is a Gouda-type cheese with a rich, rouxlike flavor married with hazelnut butter, caramel sweetness, and generous but not overbearing salt levels. Fresian sheep, milked by cheesemakers Jolanda and Gerben Bakker, graze on the island's grasses and herbs, imparting an almost imperceptible finish of fenugreek. Curiously, Terschelling gives off a beefy aroma despite being a sheep's milk Gouda and not the traditional cow.

GOES BEST WITH: Single-varietal cider. Most ciders employ a blend of apples to achieve the balance the cidermaker is going for: a few bittersharps here, a couple of bittersweets there, maybe an heirloom or two. Single-varietal ciders showcase the idiosyncrasies of a single cultivar of apple, and as such the finished cider can take a few more risks and offer up flavors that are a little more daring. You may see a single-varietal with crab apples, such as Wicksons, which produce a wild huckleberry sweet-tart cider, or one with classic Kingston Blacks that may have a sharp minerality but still carry enough balance to stand side by side with a blended cider. The cidermaker must be careful when selecting an apple to undergo this treatment; pick the wrong one and the result could be achingly sweet, or unpalatably bitter.

Terschelling has a knack for plucking out the tartness and tannins in cider and softening them until they begin to resemble sweet citrus. Think **orange marmalade** and a juicy, almost overripe **tangerine**. The cider and cheese comingle for a surprisingly long time, ending with a looooong finish of **caramelized orange peel.**

Single Varietals

Very few apples possess a natural balance of tartness, bitterness, sweetness, and flavor that makes for an appealing cider; it's why most ciders succeed only by blending different cultivars with various personalities.

So, what does it take for an apple to make it as a single-varietal cider? The bittersharp Kingston Black is the perfect example. It has acidity and bitter tannins to spare, but a strong appley flavor and enough sugar to even it all out on the back end. An apple that's a tannin bomb with no sweetness and too-subtle flavor would fail spectacularly as a single-varietal cider. Same goes for a cider made only from Red Delicious apples: all sugar, no tannins or acidity, resulting in a cider with very little depth. The list of apples that do work is a short one and includes Newtown Pippin, Golden Russet, Wickson, Baldwin, and Dabinett. It's important to note that single-varietal ciders made from the same cultivar will not all taste the same. The ripeness of the apples, yeast used, and fermentation methods all influence the final product, meaning there's a world of difference between this Cider Riot! Kingston Black over here and that Farnum Hill Kingston Black over there. And that's a good thing! A single-varietal cider that tastes like every other single-varietal cider would make for a very dull experience indeed.

CHEESE		CIDER	
## Camembert		AVAL ## Cidre Artisanal	
country of origin	*alternatives*		
France	Brie du Pommier	*country of origin*	*other suggestions*
family	Brie Fermier	France	Le Brun Brut Cidre de Bretagne
Bloomy-rind	Alemar Bent River	*style*	Loïc Raison Cidre Breton Brut
milk		Breton	
Cow			Guillet Freres Cidre Breton Brut Traditionelle

ABOUT THE CHEESE: Don't confuse Camembert with Brie. Although superficially similar, the bawdy aroma and flavors that come part and parcel with Camembert are wholly its own. The fungi-rich rind emanates pungent odors of smelly feet and ammonia, while the luscious cream inside delivers a one-two punch of cabbage and garlic. Fret not: it's much, much better than it sounds. Once a locally consumed cheese, Camembert's popularity exploded after it was included in French soldiers' rations during World War I. Pasteurized-milk Camembert isn't hard to come by, but PDO-designated (see page 86) Camembert de Normandie, made with unfiltered raw milk, is now produced by fewer dairies than ever before. We can't even get raw milk Camembert in the States because it's only aged about a month, but many producers—French and American—make stellar versions with oodles of savory character.

GOES BEST WITH: Breton cider. Southwest of Normandy, Brittany may not be as known for cider, but it still produces about 40 percent of France's total output. Typically stronger in alcohol and drier than Norman ciders, Breton ciders tend to pick up the mineral character in the region's granite-rich earth. Expect floral aromas and measured tannins from the bittersharp apples.

Camembert may come from Normandy, but matching it with cider from Brittany takes this pairing to a deliciously meaty place. The cider smooths out the cabbage in Camembert and instead evokes **charcuterie**, like a **garlicky salami**. Umami levels are off the charts, with waves of **truffles** and **alfredo sauce** washing over your palate. It's sweet, it's funky, it's fruity . . . it just sings.

QUICK BITE

A Camembert Tale

Camembert's origins are legendary . . . in that they may be closer to legend than certifiable truth. The stories tell of a woman named Marie Harel, a dairymaid living in Normandy who sheltered Abbé Charles-Jean Bonvoust during the French Revolution. The priest supposedly repaid her kindness by giving Marie the recipe for a Brie-like cheese from his homeland, which she then applied to the local raw Norman milk, packaging the finished product in round wooden containers. Marie passed the recipe down to her children, and her lineage brought the cheese to a wide audience, which prompted the town of Vimoutiers to erect a statue of her likeness. In World War II, Allied forces mistakenly bombed the town, beheading the statue in the process, but a group of dairy workers in Ohio gathered the funds to replace it as an apology. This second statue still stands today in Vimoutiers, a monument to Camembert as much as it is to the woman who may or may not have invented it.

CHEESE	CIDER
RIVER'S EDGE CHÈVRE	CHRISTIAN DROUIN
# Sunset Bay	# Cidre Pays d'Auge

country of origin	alternatives	country of origin	other suggestions
United States (Oregon)	Cypress Grove Humboldt Fog	France	E.Z. Orchards Cidre Dry
family	Capriole Sofia	*style*	Bayeux Cidre Brut Traditionnel
Bloomy-rind	Vermont Creamery	Norman	Le Père Jules Brut
milk	Bijou		Cidre de Normandie
Goat			

ABOUT THE CHEESE: If cheese could commit a crime, picking Sunset Bay from River's Edge chèvre out of a lineup would be child's play thanks to two striking physical features: a slate-colored layer of vegetable ash (see page 189) coating the rind, and a thin line of vibrant orange-red pimentón (Spanish paprika) slicing right through the middle of it. The pimentón laces the creamy and unmistakably goaty cheese with a smoky note, making Sunset Bay as complex as it is gorgeous. Letting it come to room temperature not only helps it melt on your tongue but allows the cheese's prosciutto and butter flavors to reach full strength. You want this!

GOES BEST WITH: Norman cider. Without getting too deep in the weeds, ciders from Normandy are France's oldest and funkiest, some so funky they taste and smell as if they've been sitting in an open barrel inside a horse stable for the last six years or so. Travel Normandy's picturesque Route du Cidre for a multistop journey through the Pays d'Auge, a hilly landscape crowded with orchards and farmhouses making some of the world's best ciders. Most are highly carbonated from the natural fermentation, filling your mouth with a fizzy effervescence that's playful *and* practical: it cleanses your palate after every quaff. In other words, an ace companion for a cheese-tasting session.

When Sunset Bay and Norman cider meet, the flavors they generate come in layers, usually in this order: a **peppery sizzle** up front where the apple lifts the pimentón, then a flash of sweetness from the cider, followed by a savory **leeklike** essence where the funk in the cheese and the funk in the cider meet head-on, then another glimpse of the cider's sugars before finishing with more of that rich funk. Neither the Sunset Bay nor the cider gives up an inch of its more eccentric tendencies, but the little bite of the pimentón bridges them to scrumptious effect.

CHEESE		CIDER	

JASPER HILL FARM
Harbison

ALPENFIRE CIDER
Flame

country of origin	*alternative*	*country of origin*	*other suggestions*
United States (Vermont)	Vacherin Mont d'Or	United States (Washington)	Whetstone Ciderworks Méthode Champenoise
	Jasper Hill Farm Winnimere		Orchard Hill Gold Label
family		*style*	
Bloomy-rind	Uplands Rush Creek Reserve	Méthode champenoise	Ashridge Sparkling Cider
milk			
Cow			

ABOUT THE CHEESE: The thin strip of spruce bark wrapped around a wheel of Jasper Hill's Harbison is your first clue that you're about to experience something special, a cheese a little to the left of the dial. Slicing away the top of the wheel and removing it like a lid, as the creamery suggests, reveals a gooey, puddinglike cheese fragrant with the scent of truffles. It only gets funkier from there. This is a cheese brimming with complex, gutsy flavors of stewed cabbage, mustard, garlic, horseradish, and butter, with a bit of sweetness peeking out from between the intensely savory notes. Let it come completely to room temperature for maximum spreadability.

GOES BEST WITH: Cider méthode champenoise. French and French-style ciders made in the méthode champenoise go through a much more labor-intensive process than your typical cider (see the Quick Bite for the rundown). True to name, méthode champenoise ciders resemble traditional Champagne in aroma and texture; you'll know you have one by the scent of Champagne yeast blooming out of the glass and the flurry of bubbles that disappear off your tongue like a hundred tiny whispers. They dance between dry and sweet, tart and tannic, a playful blend of green grapes and green apples.

RESULTS

An acrobatic méthode champenoise cider rolls into Harbison like a wave hitting the shore and carries its mammoth funkiness into every corner of your mouth, breaking up the rich cheese and sweetening those woody notes from the spruce bark until the combination starts to taste like fresh-picked **mulberries**. Meanwhile, the Harbison plays off the cider's pronounced yeast notes, fusing into a funky umami bomb as savory as it is delectable.

QUICK BITE

Méthode Champenoise

The traditional way to make sparkling wine is called *méthode champenoise* (named for the Champagne region in which it was invented), and it's a time-consuming practice that some cidermakers have picked up to naturally carbonate their ciders and add clarity. Here's how it works: After primary fermentation, when the yeast has converted the sugars in the apple juice to alcohol, the dry cider is bottled and given a small dose of sugar (and oftentimes yeast) to restart fermentation and create well-integrated bubbles throughout the beverage. After the bottles are capped, they're placed on a special rack, their necks angled toward the floor. Over the course of the next few weeks, the cidermaker rotates each bottle a few degrees at a time and gradually increases the angle of the bottles, causing the yeast to slowly settle at the top of the neck, just under the bottle cap. At this point, the bottles are carefully uncapped, disgorging the little glob of yeast from the bottle in a surge of pressure. The cidermaker then recaps or corks the bottles, now free of yeast, and voilà! They're ready to drink.

CHEESE		CIDER	

Idiazábal

country of origin	alternatives
Spain	Manchego
family	Etxgarai
Pressed and uncooked	Fiore Sardo
milk	
Sheep	

SIDRA TRABANCO
Sidra Avalon

country of origin	other suggestions
Spain	Sidra Brut Viuda de Angelon
style	Poma Áurea
Sparkling Spanish Sidra	Guzman Riestra Sidra Brut Nature

ABOUT THE CHEESE: The gorgeous Basque and Navarre regions on the northern edge of Spain are home to the running of the bulls in Pamplona, the rolling foothills of the western Pyrenees, and Idiazábal, a beloved sheep's milk cheese with a rich, buttery flavor and a salty finish. The nomadic shepherds who originally produced the cheese stored the wheels near the fireplace over the summer, which gave Idiazábal its smoky piquancy (and sometimes masked imperfections). You can find unsmoked varieties as well, but the smoked wheels offer a subtle woody notes rather than overwhelm with essence of campfire.

GOES BEST WITH: Sparkling Spanish sidra. Among the world's ciders, the *sidras* of Spain's Basque Country and Asturias regions (where you'll find all the orchards) stand out the loudest. Their flavors are bold, musty, and often bracingly acidic; they leave quite the impression. Most Spanish cider is not carbonated, but adding bubbles to the mix doesn't mean you won't find flavors of wet hay or aromas of acetone, or even the saltiness of a gose (see page 47). The Spaniards do have a reputation to uphold, after all.

RESULTS The zip in a sparkling Spanish sidra latches onto the smoke in Idiazábal and brings it to the surface, where it lingers pleasantly and swirls into the cider for a **funky caramel apple** sensation, while the salty cheese accentuates the cider's sugars to a level more in line with **apple brandy**. It has all the depth of a craft cocktail from an experienced mixologist, but with only two ingredients and no crowd to wade through on your way to the bar.

QUICK BITE

Smoked Cheeses

Smoking cheese is hardly a new practice. In ancient times, the most important reason for exposing cheese to smoke was to preserve it; the smoke removes surface moisture and creates a less hospitable home for harmful microorganisms to take hold. That's less of an issue now, but we still smoke cheese for the other obvious benefit: flavor. Modern cheesemakers by and large use cold-smoking methods or liquid smoke to get that distinctive taste into their products, which range from traditional Basque cheeses, such as Idiazábal, to smoked English Cheddars and smoky American blues.

Bethmale Chèvre

Sagardo Naturala

country of origin	*alternatives*	*country of origin*	*other suggestions*
France	Tieton Farm Venus	Spain	Sarasola Sagardoa
family	Central Coast Dream Weaver	*style*	Sidra Natural Riestra
Washed-rind	Twig Farm Washed Rind Wheel	Still Spanish sidra	Fanjul Sidre Natural
milk			
Goat			

ABOUT THE CHEESE: More proof that *chèvre* doesn't directly translate to "fresh, spreadable goat cheese." Before you rush out to pick up a wedge of Bethmale from your local cheesemonger, note that there two variations of this ancient Alpine-style cheese, one made from raw cow's milk and one from pasteurized goat's milk. Telling them apart visually is a snap: the cow version is yellow, and the goat is white. Bethmale chèvre offers a mild tang and a nice goaty funk that complements the cheese's sweet grass and floral flavors.

GOES BEST WITH: Still Spanish sidra. Like their carbonated brethren, still Spanish sidras are unapologetically yeasty, musty, funky, acidic, and bone dry. With no fizzy bubbles to hide behind, those flavors and characteristics are even more pronounced in still sidras, quite unlike anything else you'll ever drink. While you can throw the cider to break it and generate a quick burst of aeration (see the Quick Bite), it's perfectly enjoyable without the fanfare. Beneath the burnt rubber and peach skin aromas, the cider brims with salt and mineral qualities, along with a bracing vinegar-like acidity that lingers on your palate.

RESULTS

Pairing the French Bethmale with a still Spanish sidra is an act of neighborly kindness. On one hand, you have the cheese transforming the somewhat challenging cider into a fruitier, less acidic, much friendlier beverage that reveals some real beauty behind this "ugly duckling." On the other, the sidra tones down the goaty tang in the Bethmale and pushes up sweet **coconut milk** notes, with the apple subbing for pine-apple in a **piña colada**.

QUICK BITE

"Throwing" Spanish Sidra

Unlike most commercially produced cider, which is carbonated, Spanish sidras are still; that is, flat. The vast majority of Spanish ciders are from the Asturias region of Spain's northern coast, and if you ever get a chance to see a server "throw" or "break" an Asturian cider in person, it's well worth it (seriously, check it out on YouTube). Try it sometime. Hold the bottle as high above your head as possible and your glass as low as possible, then pour a mouthful from Point A to Point B. Good luck not getting half of it on the floor. Because these sidras are still, the journey aerates and oxidizes the liquid, generating a flurry of bubbles that briefly simulate carbonation. Drink the mouthful before it goes flat again, then repeat. It's hardly the most economical way to pour cider, but it is certainly the most eye-popping.

Paški Sir

country of origin	alternatives
Croatia	Berkswell
family	Wisconsin Sheep Dairy Coop Dante
Cooked and pressed	Bleating Heart Fat Bottom Girl
milk	
Sheep	

POVERTY LANE ORCHARDS AND FARNUM HILL CIDERS

Summer Cider

country of origin	other suggestions
United States (New Hampshire)	Wandering Aengus Wickson Crab Apple Cider
style	Redbyrd Starblossom
Tart and funky	Frederick Goussin Heritage 1900 Cuvee Tradition

ABOUT THE CHEESE: In the Adriatic Sea west of Italy, just off the Croatian mainland, there floats the narrow storm-swept island of Pag, and on this island live the 27,000-odd indigenous Paška Ovca sheep munching on whatever wild plant life they can find as they roam about. The milk of these freewheeling ewes is largely devoted to the making of a cheese known (and loved) by Croatians as Paški Sir, and the high herb distribution on the rocky island produces a rustic, lemony, leathery cheese with a tangible sheepiness that picks up notes of butterscotch as its age creeps past a year. It's usually served drizzled with olive oil, but even better paired with an effervescent beverage.

GOES BEST WITH: Tart and funky cider. Some ciders, often but not necessarily guided by wild yeasts, home in on the acidic flavors of crab apples and other bittersharp varieties like Foxwhelps and Kingston Blacks, making them accessible by backing off on their abrasive nature just enough without totally stripping them of their character (though some are so tart they're like drinking straight lime juice). How do you know the bottle of cider in your hand is a tart cider? That can be a challenge if the label doesn't specifically call it out, but you can always check with the bottle shop staff for recommendations, or ask for a Spanish sidra, as they bring the funk in spades. Our suggestions here are a great place to start.

What makes tart, funky cider work so well with Paški Sir is that the sour facets of the beverage find common ground with the cheese's lemony profile and end up unifying into a cohesive, refreshing smack of **citrus**. After the initial tongue-tingling hit, some of the sweeter shades of the Paški Sir emerge, leaving hints of **lemon meringue** and **key lime pie** on the palate. A mighty fine summertime pairing.

CHEESE	CIDER

JACOBS & BRICHFORD ## Ameribella		LOGSDON FARMHOUSE ALES ## Wilde Appel	
country of origin United States (Indiana)	*alternatives* Taleggio	*country of origin* United States (Oregon)	*other suggestions* Oyster River Winegrowers Wildman
family Washed-rind	Tulip Tree Foxglove Durrus	*style* Wild	Big Hill Farmhouse
milk Cow			Dragon's Head Wild Fermented

ABOUT THE CHEESE: A Midwestern take on northern Italian Taleggio. Named for its creator Matthew Brichford's great-grandmother America Arabella, Ameribella isn't a cheese easily forgotten, and not just for its unusual squashed brick shape. Piercing the orange rind (a hallmark of the brine brushed over the cheese) reveals a soft, sticky, custardy paste and a pungent funk that clues you in on how this whole experience is going to go down in your mouth. Mustard and chanterelles come through strongest, with a sour bite and salty finish.

GOES BEST WITH: Wild cider. In the beer world, ales soured through exposure to wild yeast and bacteria like *Brettanomyces* and *Lactobacillus* are treasured for their fearless embrace of the tang. Wild-fermented ciders offer the same flirtation with funk, but even more so thanks to the presence of wild yeast on the apples themselves. Cider being cider, the resulting liquid is usually a little juicier than its malt-born rival, with some lively tropical notes.

A good wild cider and Ameribella is a funk-on-funk soirée that somehow smooths out the cheese's more astringent edges, letting the tartness in the cider hoist up Ameribella's creamy character. We got big **lemon curd** flavors and **salty piña colada** from this pairing, fruity acid balanced by thick cream.

CHEESE		CIDER	

COWGIRL CREAMERY
Red Hawk

DOC'S DRAFT HARD CIDERS
Dry Hopped Cider

country of origin	*alternatives*	*country of origin*	*other suggestions*
United States (California)	Marin French Cheese Schloss	United States (New York)	Tieton Cider Works Yakima Valley Dry Hopped Cider
family	Crown Finish Caves Trifecta	*style*	Oliver's at the Hop
Triple-crème, washed-rind	Soumaintrain	Hopped	Reverend Nat's Hallelujah Hopricot
milk			
Cow			

ABOUT THE CHEESE: Washed-rind triple-crèmes are a rare breed, a clue that Cowgirl Creamery's Red Hawk is already something special before you even take a taste. The *Brevibacterium linens* present in the environment at the creamery's original location in Point Reyes grows on the rind and tints it a pinkish ochre; it's also responsible for the cheese's distinctive footlike pungency that may scare off the meek. Beneath that stinky rind, Red Hawk's soft ivory paste houses rich flavors of bacon fat and beef tallow, butter and salt, all melding lusciously in your mouth with a velvety smoothness.

GOES BEST WITH: Hopped cider. Hops aren't exclusive to the domain of beer, but their use in cider is still in its infant stages, so what's available to purchase is all over the map in terms of balance. While some ciders are so infused with the essence of hops that they completely dwarf any apple character, certain varieties of hops, used judiciously, offer juicy citrus and woodsy flavors and aromas that complement cider instead of clashing with it.

The salty/sweet interplay that transpires when you pair a hopped cider with Red Hawk is not unlike a **salt-rimmed margarita**: big salinity up front, clinging to the sweetness of the beverage and accentuating it, followed by a twinkle of **lime zest**. Despite the emphasized sugars, the pairing finishes dry, like **black tea**, and any perfumey pine notes from the hops vanish in the wake of Red Hawk's funky rind.

QUICK BITE

Ye Olde Hop Picking

Prior to the advent of mechanization, hops had to be picked by hand, a time-consuming process requiring legions of workers in late summer/early fall. To entice potential hop pickers out from the cities to the more rural farmlands, hop growers placed advertisements offering all manner of perks for joining the labor force, including free whiskey, nightly dances, swimming holes, clean tents or "hopper huts," even an evangelist on Sundays. Hop picking brought together a multicultural pastiche of workers from many different backgrounds; in the Pacific Northwest, you'd see members of Native American tribes picking hops alongside European immigrants, Chinese laborers, and entire low-income families brought in on the Hop Special train from Portland to Independence, Oregon. Workers were paid per pound of collected hops, and the most consummate pickers could earn as much in a six-day work week as they could in a month at a local factory, if so motivated.

MISSOURI GREEN DIRT FARM
Dirt Lover

country of origin	*alternatives*
United States (Missouri)	Nancy's Camembert
	Perail
family	Shepherd's Way Hidden Falls
Bloomy-rind	
milk	
Sheep	

BLUE MOUNTAIN CIDER COMPANY
Cherry Hard Apple Cider

country of origin	*other suggestions*
United States (Oregon)	Anthem Cherry
style	Northville Winery Crimson Dew
Cherry	
	Original Sin Cherry Tree

ABOUT THE CHEESE: Cut a wedge out of this semisoft Brie-like cheese from Missouri's Green Dirt Farm and you'll find a striking dark border running just beneath the soft rind. That's vegetable ash, applied in the style of ash-coated French cheeses, such as Valençay or Saint-Maure de Touraine. The ash imparts a faint cedar woodiness to the cheese's grassy, buttery flavor and isn't just there for show: it neutralizes the pH in the rind, helping it form properly (read more about ash in the Quick Bite). Beneath the ash is a creamy ivory ring with a luscious mouthfeel, offering a pleasing contrast to the cheese's drier, crumbly core and sheepy tang.

GOES BEST WITH: Cherry cider. Cherry ciders can go wrong quickly; they often push the sugars so far that it's like drinking liquefied candy. When done well, they start to manifest the tart, acidic qualities of sour cherry ales (krieks), landing on the palate with the mild sweetness of homemade fruit leather and a perfect balance between apple and cherry. The average cherry ciders use about a pound of cherries per gallon of apple cider, usually with the pits included to infuse the beverage with a touch of tannins behind the fruity punch.

RESULTS

That pit-driven bitterness attaches itself to the similarly bitter facets of Dirt Lover, canceling them out and leaving you with a lovely taste of **mushrooms cooked in a red wine reduction,** or a **beef bourguignon cooked with loads of onions and tomatoes.** After the savory notes hit, the sweet cherries rise up at the end, as if capping off a hearty supper with a nip of brandy.

QUICK BITE

Vegetable Ash

One of farmers' earliest known methods of protecting cheese from insects and microscopic critters was to rub the ash off the bottom of a pot placed over an open fire after the milk inside was warmed, and then apply it to the outside of the cheese. Later, cheesemakers switched to burning vine clippings, though in modern times it's all charred vegetable matter. Not only does the ash alter the pH levels in the cheese's surface, but it dries it out as well, helping it age longer without succumbing to undesirable molds. And frankly, it cloaks cheeses in a stunning garment (or in the case of such cheeses as Humboldt Fog, a gorgeous gray belt) to catch the eye.

VINTAGE CHEESE OF MONTANA
Mountina

CROWN VALLEY BREWING
Blackberry Cider

country of origin	alternatives	country of origin	other suggestions
United States (Montana)	Fontina Val d'Aosta	United States (Missouri)	2 Towns Made Marion
	Central Coast		Bishop Crackberry
family	Holey Cow	style	Bold Rock Blackberry
Alpine-style washed-rind	Parish Hill Vermont Herdsman	Blackberry/marionbery	
milk			
Cow			

ABOUT THE CHEESE: Cheesemaking is in Vintage Cheese cofounder Darryl Heap's blood. A third-generation cheese-maker like his brother Dwayne and a Kraft Foods grunt at the age of 13, he honed his chops on cheeses that probably never saw the insides of a discriminating cheesemonger's display case. Now at the helm of his own business in Boze-man, Montana, a state with a once-thriving dairy industry that's suffered in recent decades, Heap's got a stunner on his hands. Mountina is a brined Alpine-style cheese similar to fontina that deftly balances a mouth-coating creaminess with the hearty warmth of French onion soup, with a pinch of funk and grass tossed in. Be sure to serve it closer to room tem-perature to let the menagerie of flavors come out to play.

GOES BEST WITH: Marionberry or blackberry cider. As with all ciders, whether or not they're teaming up with other flavors, a little sugar goes a long way. Some cideries seem to take the addition of a second fruit as an invitation to crank up the sweetness and obliterate the line between cider and Kool-Aid. But when approached with a little finesse, these multifruit ciders can really deliver something special, com-plex, and most of all, fun.

A good blackberry or marionberry cider needs to balance the delicate profile of the apples with more assertive berries, and that balance is best achieved with actual fruit, not an

extract. It should be alive with the flavors of—shocking!—
fresh-picked berries, and as a result, offer a modicum of tartness (if it's full-on sour, then it almost surely was inoculated
with special bacteria or yeast).

Pair blackberry cider with Mountina and your reward is a **peanut butter and jelly
sandwich**. No joke. This combination is so evocative of creamy peanut butter and
blackberry jelly spread over slices of unobtrusive white bread, you'll swear it came
in a plastic lunchbox.

CHEESE		CIDER	
ROTH		**CORNISH ORCHARDS**	
# Prairie Sunset		# Pear Cider	
country of origin	*alternatives*	*country of origin*	*other suggestions*
United States (Wisconsin)	Mimolette	England	Uncle John's Apple Pear
	Edam	*style*	
family	Pavé du Nord	Pear	Fox Barrel Pacific Pear
Washed-curd			Blacke's Grizzly Pear
milk			
Cow			

ABOUT THE CHEESE: Traffic-cone orange and riddled with tiny eyes, Prairie Sunset is a beauty to behold and certainly worthy of its evocative name. The original recipe is based on French Mimolette (see page 44), but beyond the obvious visual and textural similarities (both use annatto to get that dashing cantaloupe hue, both are somewhat waxy and chewy), God is, as they say, in the detail. Whereas Mimolette tastes of hazelnuts and well-marbled beef, Prairie Sunset is subtly sweet, a cross between garden-fresh carrots, clotted cream, and salted caramel.

GOES BEST WITH: Pear cider. Pear juice is a great choice not only to inflect some natural pear flavor into an ordinary apple cider, but to sweeten it: pears contain sorbitol, which doesn't turn to alcohol like most other sugars. There are no specifications as to the percentage of apple juice vs. pear juice that can be used in a pear cider, so the bottle you pick up may taste strongly of apple and only a hint of pear somewhere off in the distance, or like drinking straight pear juice with no apple in sight. Avoid the mass-market stuff, as their monstrous sweetness will blow out this pairing.

When consumed with pear cider, Prairie Sunset suddenly becomes a much saltier cheese, to the point that it's sufficient to balance the sugars in the beverage while drawing out some fascinating sweet or savory notes. Like, for example, the deep caramelization of **oven-roasted beets in balsamic dressing**, or **kettle corn**. There's also a really satisfying equalization of weight and texture between the cheese and the cider you just have to experience to appreciate.

Castelmagno

TWO RIVERS CIDER CO.
Huckleberry Cider

country of origin	*alternatives*
Italy	Leonardo
	Castelrosso
family	
Blue	
milk	
Cow	

country of origin	*other suggestions*
United States (California)	Wildcraft Elderberry Perry
style	Harvest Moon Red Barn Raspberry
Berry	Downeast Cider House Wild Berry

ABOUT THE CHEESE: Fun fact about Castelmagno: Although technically a blue cheese, as it's inoculated with the blue *penicillium* mold, oftentimes there isn't a trace of blue to be found in it. A very old cheese going back at least to the thirteenth century, it's now PDO/DOP protected (see page 86) and made in just three towns (Castelmagno, Monterosso Grana, and Pradleves) in Italy's Piedmont region. The cheese is finely milled before it's pressed, which gives it a crumbly texture. Tangy yogurt dominates the flavor, with a salty backbone and an earthy funk lying just beneath the surface.

GOES BEST WITH: Berry cider. Pears are the most common fruit to augment apple-based ciders, but berries—particularly elderberries, raspberries, lingonberries, and huckleberries—introduce vinous aromas and a measure of tartness that fuses with apples in unique and playful ways. The key is balance: finding a way to prominently showcase the myriad facets of the featured berry without smothering the apples' individuality.

RESULTS

Castelmagno and berry ciders both embody some degree of natural tartness, but together their tang ducks into the background, letting the cheese's earthier notes come out to play. Simultaneously, the sugars in the cider bubble to the surface, making the Castelmagno taste and feel extra creamy. The pairing finishes with some of those mouth-drying tannins in the apples and berries, with a dash of salt.

QUICK BITE

The Loopy World of Cider and Taxes

As it relates to cider, the US tax code has long suffered under arcane regulations and baffling categorizations, such as designating ciders as wines and increasing taxes on ciders carbonated over a certain percentage, ciders with an alcohol content of 7% or higher, and ciders made with any fruit other than apples. This resulted in a lot of low-carbonated ciders watered down to avoid crossing the 7% threshold. Insanity!

Recent updates to the code have finally injected some common sense, cutting taxes and making ciders with multiple fruits much more financially feasible. But over in the United Kingdom, they're waiting for some good ol' tax reform. Carbonated ciders between 5.5% and 8.5% are punished hardest, incurring nearly seven times the excise duty of a still cider below 7.5% ABV or a carbonated one under 5.5%. What does that mean? You guessed it: lots of still ciders, and bubbly ciders below 5.5%. But don't seal your bottle of still cider with a mushroom cork: that automatically bumps you up into the carbonated rates. Because with a tax code this archaic, why not?

CHEESE		CIDER	
FROMAGERIE AGOUR # Arpea		**TIETON CIDER WORKS** # Spice Route	
country of origin France	*alternatives* Lark's Meadow Farms Alto Valle Ovelha	*country of origin* United States (Washington)	*other suggestions* Vermont Cider Co. Wassail
family Washed-rind		*style* Spiced	D's Wicked Cider Co. Baked Apple
milk Sheep			Rekorderlig Spiced Apple

ABOUT THE CHEESE: The woody, wooly lanolin flavor in many sheep's milk cheeses can make them difficult to pair unless you find a beverage that either masks those notes or finds a way to complement them. Although it's a Pyrenees/ Basque Country cheese like Ossau-Iraty, Arpea from Fromagerie Agour lacks the wool sweater overtones in those cheeses, possibly because it's not aged nearly as long as the harder cheeses the region is known for. Instead, Arpea is much closer to a milder cow's milk Taleggio: a little sweet, a little funky, with hints of garlic scapes and a crunchy washed rind (more on that in the Quick Bite).

GOES BEST WITH: Spiced cider. Spiced ciders harken to the holidays, where cinnamon, cloves, nutmeg, and allspice find their way into everything from apple pie to mulled wine. This is the cider equivalent of Belgian witbier (see page 49), except these pie spices are more pronounced than the coriander and orange peel ever are in wits. You'll often pick up a brown sugar sweetness in these cider, further pushing them into dessert territory.

RESULTS

Something as assertively flavored as spiced cider is never going to give up much ground when it comes to aligning it with a cheese, nor will you find much success pairing it with cheese that's equally aggressive: you're more likely to create a jumbled, chaotic mess than come within a thousand miles of balance. Instead, the trick to pairing spiced cider is to match it with a cheese that takes all those big aromatic spices and quietly supports the group in its entirety. That's where Arpea shines, taking spiced cider from liquid apple pie to a new place, and that place is somewhere halfway between **cola** and **birch beer**, halfway between **Dr Pepper** and **cream soda**.

QUICK BITE

Surface Crystals

Ever open a shrink-wrapped aged Cheddar and find it covered in white blotches? Don't toss it in the trash thinking it's mold, and don't assume it's salt left over from the brining/washing process, because it's not. That's calcium lactate, lactic acid reacting to the calcium in the cheese, and it usually signifies a flavorful product. What about washed-rind cheeses such as Arpea, whose rinds can be gritty and crunchy? That's a combination of ikaite (calcium carbonate) and struvite (magnesium ammonium phosphate), and they're both totally edible. That said, we're by no means sticklers about eating the rind on every cheese, so if the grittiness bothers you, go ahead and cut it away.

CHEESE		CIDER	

OBERE MUHLE
Chiriboga

ARGUS CIDERY
Ciderkin

country of origin	*alternatives*	*country of origin*	*other suggestions*
Germany	Swissmathier Simme Bleu	United States (Texas)	Aspall Cyderkyn
family	Kāpiti Kikorangi	*style*	The Cider Mill Ciderkin
Blue	Roth Buttermilk Blue	Ciderkin	
milk			
Cow			

ABOUT THE CHEESE: It's not every day an Ecuadorian moves to Bad Oberdorf, Germany, to join the Obere Muhle creamery and revive a century-old blue cheese recipe meant to rival Roquefort, but that's exactly what Arturo Chiraboga did in 1997. What sets Chiriboga apart from other blues is that the mold is not introduced by inoculating the milk, but by dipping long needles in the mold solution and impaling the young cheese wheels with them. The resulting cheese has subtle blue mold flavors, more a blend of salted cream and cultured butter than the big mold funk of a giant like Stilton. A great starter blue!

GOES BEST WITH: Ciderkin. This little-known style of cider was traditionally made by pouring water over the leftover apple solids after the first pressing (hence its other common name, "water-cider") letting it sit a day or two, then pressing it again and fermenting the thin juice. Being low in alcohol and often augmented with additives such as molasses and spices meant ciderkin could be consumed by colonial children while adults downed the stronger stuff. It's rare these days, but you'll sometimes find it on tap in local cideries, and Texas's Argus Cidery nationally distributes a Granny Smith–tart, spritzy version with a nice straightforward apple profile.

RESULTS

Although ciderkin and Chiriboga don't produce a completely new rainbow of flavors like most of our pairings, they complement each other so harmoniously that we had to tell you about it. While the cheese softens the ciderkin's bite, leaving a Gala-like **apple essence** in the forefront, the beverage's acid lifts up the heavy Chiriboga, sweetening it substantially and flooding your palate with its irresistible **butteriness**. Ciderkin really makes this cheese sing, so tracking down a bottle will be well worth the effort.

NETTLE MEADOW
Kunik

country of origin	*alternatives*
United States (New York)	Vermont Creamery Cremont
family	Coach Farm Triple Cream
Triple-crème, bloomy-rind	Woolwich Dairy Triple Créme Goat Brie
milk	
Goat, with cow cream	

TILTED SHED CIDERWORKS
Barred Rock Barrel-Aged Cider

country of origin	*other suggestions*
United States (California)	Potter's Craft Oak Barrel Reserve
style	Bad Seed Bourbon Barrel Reserve
Barrel-aged	Stem Cidery Le Chêne

ABOUT THE CHEESE: One way of rounding out goat milk's defining tanginess while boosting its butterfat content is to mix in a little cow's milk cream, and that's exactly what Nettle Meadow Farm in the Adirondacks of upstate New York does with its pucks of luscious Kunik. Silky and spreadable, it pulls off the admirable feat of letting both the cow's cream and the goat's milk shine without obliterating the other, so you end up with a cheese with the body of thick cream and the flavors of whole milk, mushrooms, and that lively goat twang.

GOES BEST WITH: Barrel-aged cider. Barrel-aging cider accomplishes three things. First, it gives new life to barrels that would otherwise be destroyed after the liquor or wine originally aged in them made its way into bottles. Second, it gives young ciders time to mellow out and mature, smoothing down sharp corners for a more even beverage. And third, it introduces layers of complexity imparted by the wood and whatever liquid previously occupied the barrels. Rye whiskey barrels work especially well with cider, as the spicy rye adds a note of apple-friendly cinnamon, a perfect companion for the vanilla coming off the oak.

Let Kunik and a barrel-aged cider get acquainted and you'll see that vanilla note magnified in a big way. Right behind the initial **vanilla cream** essence you'll catch a glimpse of the salt in the cheese, finishing with **roasted cashews** and bitter **apple skin.**

QUICK BITE

Txoxt

Should you find yourself traveling through the Basque Country of northern Spain between late January and April, make a point of visiting one of its *sagardotegis* (cider houses), for a hearty meal. Not long after sitting down and tucking into salt cod omelets and bloody-rare steak, you'll hear someone shout "Txoxt!" (pronounced "choach"). Follow the guests as they push away from the table and hurry excitedly to one of the *kupelas* (giant casks) lining the cellar. You'll see a bucket resting about five or six feet from the front of the kupela and guests queuing up next to it, a sign of what's to come. When the cidermaker opens the valve, tart, funky Spanish sidra will arc from the barrel toward the bucket, and if the first person in the line is deft enough, the cider will never reach that destination. Instead, it should land in the guest's glass, angled so the cider hits the side to agitate the liquid and provide a momentary illusion of carbonation, the same concept as breaking Spanish sidra (see page 177). After collecting a few fingers' worth, the guest will step aside, allowing the next person in line, crouched with the glass over the bucket, to pick up where they left off, and so on through the queue. Perhaps not the most efficient or cleanest way of getting your cider from cask to mouth, but certainly the most fun.

Don't want to journey all the way to Spain just to try txoxting for yourself? Visit the Black Twig Cider House in Durham, North Carolina, which replicates the experience reasonably well from a barrel set into the wall.

Bleu des Basques

ERIC BORDELET
Poiré Authentique

country of origin	*alternatives*
France	Shepherd's Way Big Woods Blue
family	Beenleigh Blue
Blue	Hook's Little Boy Blue
milk	
Sheep	

country of origin	*other suggestions*
France	Gwatkin Farmhouse Perry
style	Pacory Poiré Domfront
Perry/Poiré	Hallets Perry

ABOUT THE CHEESE: Blue novices, pay attention: here's another gateway cheese for you! Much milder and fruitier than the average blue, with barely a murmur of tang or funk from the blue-gray mold, this "blue of the Basque region" is a smooth, accessible cheese that nonetheless carries plenty of subtle grass and Pyrenees character to please even the most jaded palate. Don't worry if your wedge starts "weeping" oil on the surface not long after pulling it from the fridge: that's just an indicator of the luscious high-fat sheep's milk within.

GOES BEST WITH: Perry/Poiré. Not to be confused with pear cider (see the Quick Bite), perry is the primo showcase for fermented pear juice; no apples were harmed in the making of this beverage. Pears naturally contain more unfermentable sugars (such as sorbitol) than apples, so there will almost always be a brightness and a sweetness to perry, but some producers coax more bitter tannins from the fruit, so don't make the mistake of thinking they're all the same. Eric Bordelet's Poiré Authentique is an absolute marvel of vibrant spiced pear character and cinnamon warmth, a slam dunk with just about any cheese. American perry is a much harder beast to track down, simply because we don't have nearly the perry pear production as France or England, so if you have a local option, by all means seek it out!

RESULTS

A good perry takes Bleu des Basques on the express train to Dessertville. The sweetness in the perry clings to the sweetness in the cheese but doesn't tamp down Bleu's salinity at all, so you end up with **vanilla ice cream** paired with **butterscotch** and **salted toffee**. Bleu des Basques's mild funk doesn't fizzle out either; instead it connects with the fermented pear notes at the end with a welcome transition out of the sweetness. It's just beautiful.

QUICK BITE

Perry vs. Pear Cider

Put simply, perry is a fermented beverage made from pears, and "pear cider" can be made with any combination of pear juice, pear juice concentrate, and apple juice. Perry has a longstanding tradition in England and France's Normandy region, where orchards routinely maintained the large trees growing the varieties of gritty pears that make for a horrible snack but which contain the right combination of sugars, acids, and tannins to carry the fermentation into an elegant alcoholic luxury. But the difficulties in growing and fermenting these pears, coupled with an increasing demand for cider, drove down the perry market . . . until recently. Now demand is skyrocketing and perrymakers are struggling to keep up. In comes pear cider, which makes do with little to no genuine perry pear juice, to pick up the slack while the newly planted and notoriously slow-to-fruit perry trees mature. Today, plenty of great pear ciders worthy of your hard-earned bucks are available, so don't dismiss them by any means; just know they're a different beast and should be treated as such.

CHEESE		CIDER	
L'AMUSE		**FINNRIVER FARM & CIDERY**	
# Signature Gouda		# Apple Wine	

country of origin	*alternatives*	*country of origin*	*other suggestions*
Holland	Rembrandt Extra-Aged	United States (Washington)	Earle Estates Meadery Apple Enchantment
family	Marieke Aged Gouda		Chankaska Creek
Gouda	Caves of Faribault Jeffs' Select Gouda	*style*	Apple Wine
milk		Apple Wine	1911 McIntosh Classic Apple Wine
Cow			

ABOUT THE CHEESE: Fromagerie L'Amuse is actually a cheese retailer/importer/exporter based in Amsterdam, but its influence on the Dutch cheese industry bears mentioning. The crown jewel in the company's close relationship with the Cono and Lutjewinkel cheesemakers must certainly be its Signature Gouda, a surefire hit on any cheese plate and a slam dunk with higher alcohol beverages. L'Amuse co-owner Betty Koster selects every wheel of Gouda before it's aged in a warmer, higher humidity environment than most Dutch Gouda. The result is a deep amber cheese packed with crunchy tyrosine crystals and pronounced butterscotch, roasted hazelnut, and dark caramel flavors, so massive that they seem to fill your entire mouth after just a nibble.

GOES BEST WITH: Apple wine. What happens when you take cider and jack it up with additional sugars before fermenting? You get apple wine, cider's boozier sibling that isn't afraid to boast an ABV well above the 10% mark. Apple wines seek out the core flavors in cider and crank the volume to 11; that means lots of sweet honey, raisins, and pears behind the big alcohol on the nose.

Gouda, especially one as attention-grabbing as L'Amuse, needs something potent, such as apple wine, to stand up to its bold palate-assailing richness. This is a pairing that uses the concept of contrasting to great effect, bouncing between sweet and salty like **buttered popcorn** with a **drizzle of caramel** and a **handful of peanuts**. So, **Fiddle Faddle**. The **roasted nut** notes stretch out into a long, satisfying finish, a lingering good-bye to a saturation of intense, deeply comforting flavors.

QUICK BITE

Tyrosine Crystals

We've covered crystals that grow on the surface of cheeses (see page 196), but let's briefly talk about the really fun ones: those crunchy little sweet/salty pockets stashed away in long-aged cheeses like gold nuggets in a mine. These crystals start out as caches of the amino acid tyrosine in the form of proteins, which slowly break down and dissolve, creating crystals until all the tyrosine in the area is used up. Tyrosine crystals should not be seen as a flaw; they're an indication that the cheese has aged properly, and the textural contrast is so unique and desirable that judges at the annual American Cheese Society (page 99) competition have started evaluating ideal distribution in such cheeses as Gouda and Parmesan. Tyrosine: so hot right now.

SPRING BROOK FARM
Ashbrook

CLOS SARAGNAT
L'Original Cidre de Glace

country of origin	*alternatives*
United States (Vermont)	Morbier
	Leelanau Raclette
family	Oka
Washed-rind	
milk	
Cow	

country of origin	*other suggestions*
Canada	Eden Heirloom Blend
	Neige Premiere
style	Slyboro Ciderhouse
Ice cider	Ice Harvest Special Reserve

ABOUT THE CHEESE: Ashbrook is proof positive that just because something has been made one way for years, it doesn't mean it can't be improved upon. After award-winning cheesemaker Jeremy Stephenson received requests for a local cheese in the style of French Morbier, he spent most of 2014 fine-tuning his recipe, and now we have the gorgeous Ashbrook to thank him for. Its defining characteristic is the line of blue-gray vegetable ash running through the center of the chiffon-colored cheese, added by slicing the just-formed wheel in half like a bagel. Rich and smooth, Ashbrook delivers earthy clay-and-mushroom flavors that morph into a lactic, fermented-fruit sweetness.

GOES BEST WITH: Ice cider. Of course a French Canadian winemaker invented ice cider. By leaving certain species of apples on the tree into the winter months and letting them freeze for a few chilly Quebecan nights, just as grapes are left to freeze on the vine to make ice wine, Christian Barthomeuf forced the water in the apples to separate from the sugar, resulting in juice that ferments out to much higher alcohol levels. Ice cider takes an apple's inherent acidity, sweetness, and tartness and concentrates it so magnificently, so intensely, that just a tiny sip detonates on your palate into an entire orchard's worth of flavor.

RESULTS

A rich, supple cheese like Ashbrook may seem to call out for something light and fizzy to cut through the fat, but we found the vividly sweet allure of ice cider took this pairing right past the realm of over the top and into outer space. Consuming them together is like eating a soft, **butter-rich pastry**. As the cheese mingles with the cider, its earthy flavors smooth into **apple fruit leather and caramel**, leaving behind all traces of fungal funk. It's so luscious, so decadent, that you may only last a few bites before you experience flavor overload, but what a glorious few bites that will be.

QUICK BITE

Cryoextraction vs. Cryoconcentration

You've read about how ice cider came to be, by letting apples freeze on the tree, thaw, and freeze again, causing ice crystals in the apple flesh to form and break, form and break, until the sugar accumulates at the surface. That's called cryoextraction, and while it makes for a great story, it's not the most practical way of getting the water and sugar in an apple to separate. By far the more common method of making ice cider is by harvesting apples in the fall and pressing them as you would normally, but then freezing the juice in a process called cryoconcentration. That doesn't mean you have to stick the juice in a commercial freezer: if you live far enough north, you can just pour it into ice trays, set it outside, and let Mother Nature handle it.

## Part III

BEYOND THE BOOK: CONTINUED EXPLORATIONS

FINAL THOUGHTS

It doesn't sound like a lot, 75 cheeses and a beer, wine, or cider to go with each. Knock that out in a couple of dedicated weekends, how hard could it be?

It took us years, *years* of tasting to get these final 75 into your hands. We tasted and retasted and tasted some more . . . and then tasted again. Some pairings arrived immediately (clothbound Cheddar with English semidry cider comes to mind), as if pulled straight from heaven's fridge. Some took months of failure (looking at you, Lancashire) before finally striking gold. It was a long, spirited, meandering, grueling, thrilling journey jam-packed with unpredictable twists and turns. A potboiler novel minus the murder and steamy love affairs.

It wasn't just two guys scarfing down gobs of gourmet cheese, chugging gallons of beer, draining cases of quality wine, and sending entire orchards worth of cider down our throats, though. We did pick up a few things along the way we didn't know going in:

- **Not only are there exceptions to the rules, but exceptions are the norm.** Let's pick on Lancashire again. Hardly the most assertive cheese around, it begs for a comparable cohort of similarly light stature. We must have tried that sucker with two dozen different beers, wines, and ciders before finally finding a mate in the unlikeliest of places: rauchbier, as aggressively flavored a drink as you're going to find. Never could have seen that coming. And time after time, we'd have a cheese from one location and a bottle of something from the same area, thinking a regional match was a shoo-in, only to discover that its most interesting foil was a beverage from a completely different part of the globe. So, as we said early on in this book, when you're setting off on your own to find brand new pairings, treat the *comparable/contrasting/regional* guidelines as exactly that: guidelines, not guardrails.

- **Variances within examples of the same style of beer/wine/cider from different breweries/wineries/cideries don't change the final outcome all that much.** If you're fretting over whether to pair that Lorelei with a hefeweizen from Franziskaner or one from Schneider Weisse, relax. We got nearly the same result with both. As long as it's true to style, it'll work no matter who made it.

- **Washed-rind cheeses play nice with wine and cider; with beer, it's a scuffle.** We only ended up pairing one beer with a washed-rind cheese. Over and over, we found that malt and hops have a tendency to pull out rude, unpalatable flavors from a shocking number of washed-rind varieties, which doesn't happen with other categories of cheese.

- **Cider is unquestionably the easiest beverage to pair with cheese, but the highest highs and lowest lows come from beer and wine.** During the sessions in which we were pairing cheeses with ciders, we were never worried we wouldn't find at least one combination that really sang. Cider's—even dry cider's—residual sugars and inherent apple flavor are the perfect foil for salty, nutty, creamy foods like cheese. But the biggest flavors, the most interesting and rewarding ones that made us stand up and clap our hands and point down at the table and shout, "Pure magic!", those came far more frequently with beer and wine. Inversely, the pairings that absolutely bombed? Also beer and wine, more often than not.

- **We don't always agree on which pairing works best.** A few times throughout the pairing process, one of us went bananas over the way a particular cheese tasted with a particular beer, wine, or cider, while the other scratched his head and shrugged. It wasn't often, but it happened. It's just the way the human palate works, and why when you go to a wine tasting or one of those websites where people can post their tasting notes on wine or beer, you'll *never* see two individuals experience the exact same beverage in the exact same way. It's guaranteed you won't pick out all the same flavors we did when you try these combinations, but that's okay. What's important is that you don't try to force yourself into thinking you taste what we taste. There is no wrong answer; your interpretation is your interpretation, and this book is all about getting you to think about the *idea* of consuming cheese and beer/wine/cider together so you're confident and comfortable enough to give your own pairings a spin.

We hope you enjoyed traveling with us on this delicious, occasionally pungent expedition, and that you actually tried some of our suggestions. If it sparked a little friendly debate about what works better with what, all the better, but heed our one last piece of advice: Don't take it too seriously. Life has enough tedium of its own to bother dragging down something as joyous as eating cheese and drinking alcohol into pedantic snobbery. Not every cheese needs to be redolent of gym socks and cabbage; it's okay to enjoy crowd-pleasers like Cheddar, okay to like sweeter ciders, okay to drink cheaper wines, okay to prefer lighter beers. It's all delicious, and more important than *what* you're consuming is *with whom* you're consuming it. Cheese and alcohol are some of life's great social equalizers: they require no expertise to appreciate, and they become infinitely more enjoyable when shared with even a single other human being, whether that individual is a seasoned gourmand or a total rookie to the world of finer foods. This book was our way of sharing these experiences with you, and we look forward to sharing them with you in person, should our paths cross. We hope they do.

—STEVE JONES & ADAM LINDSLEY

ADDITIONAL CHEESE AND BEVERAGE PAIRINGS

Seventy-five pairings not enough to appease your insatiable appetite? Lucky you, we've got loads of runner-up choices, the ones that made a big impression but were just edged out by the pairings we ended up featuring. Second-tier or not, you won't go wrong with anything here!

beer

CHEESE	BEER
Aged Cheddar	Victory Pilsner
Bucheron	Cascade Apricot Ale
Cheshire	Occidental Kolsch
Comté	Rochefort 6
French Camembert	Russian River Supplication
Jasper Hill Willoughby	Green Bench Les Grisettes
Mahon Reserva	Ayinger Oktober Fest-Märzen
Mimolette	Ayinger Celebrator
Mt. Townsend Creamery Off Kilter	Hoegaarden Wit
Rogue Smokey Blue	Firestone Walker Union Jack

wine

CHEESE	WINE
Shepherd's Way Big Woods Blue	W & J Graham's 10 Year Old Tawny Port
Époisses	Ayres Perspective Pinot Noir
Gabietou	L'Ecole No. 41 Sémillon
Morbier	Gewürztraminer
Munster	Domaine de Fenouillet Muscat de Beaumes de Venise
Parmigiano-Reggiano	Cleto Chiarli Lambrusco Secco del Fondatore
Patacabra	Skouras Saint George Aghiorghitiko Nemea
Pecorino Sardo	Lava Cap Matagrano Sangiovese
Tomme de Savoie	Marc Pesnot Domaine de La Sénéchalerie Folle Blanche
Uplands Dairy Private Reserve	Division Gamay Noir "Cru"

cider

CHEESE	CIDER
Jacobs & Brichford Ameribella	Cider Riot! Burncider
Willamette Valley Creamery Boerenkaas	Wandering Aengus Bloom
Clothbound Cheddar	Swift Hard Apple
Fresh Chevre	Anthem Cherry
Garrotxa	North Idaho Logger
Manchego	Baird & Dewar Silvestra
Cowgirl Creamery Red Hawk	Sidra Avalon
River's Edge Chèvre Sunset Bay	Isastegi Sagardo Naturala
Tirslinger	Woodbox Pippin
Capriole Wabash Cannonball	Division Gamay Noir "Cru"

RECOMMENDED READING

Atlas of American Artisan Cheese by Jeffrey P. Roberts (Chelsea Green)

The Beer Bible by Jeff Alworth (Workman Publishing)

Beer & Cheese by Ben Vinken and Michel Van Tricht (Lannoo)

The Book of Cheese by Liz Thorpe (Flatiron Books)

Cider: Hard & Sweet by Ben Watson (Countryman Press)

Cider Made Easy by Jeff Alworth (Chronicle Books)

Cheddar: A Journey into the Heart of America's Most Iconic Cheese by Gordon Edgar (Chelsea Green)

Cheese: A Connoisseur's Guide to the World's Best by Max McCalman & David Gibbons (Clarkson Potter)

Cheese & Beer by Janet Fletcher (Andrews McMeel)

The Cheeses of Vermont by Henry Tewksbury (Countryman Press)

Craft Cider: How to Turn Apples into Alcohol by Jeff Smith (Countryman Press)

Culture Magazine

The Great American Ale Trail by Christian DeBenedetti (Running Press)

Guide to Cheeses of the World by Roland Barthelemy and Arnaud Sperat-Czar (Hachette)

The Guide to West Coast Cheeses by Sasha Davies (Timber Press)

Laura Werlin's Cheese Essentials (Stewart, Tabori & Chang)

The Oxford Companion to Cheese (Oxford University Press)

Pacific Northwest Cheese: A History by Tami Parr (Oregon State University Press)

Reinventing the Wheel by Bronwen and Francis Percival (University of California Press)

Taste Buds & Molecules by François Chartier (Houghton Mifflin Harcourt)

The Wine Bible by Karen MacNeil (Workman Publishing)

The World Atlas of Wine by Hugh Johnson and Jancis Robinson (Mitchell Beazley)

The World Encyclopedia of Cheese by Juliet Harbutt (Hermes House)

INDEX

Note: *Specific cheeses* are listed individually.

For information about permission to reproduce selections from this book, write to
Permissions, The Countryman Press, 500 Fifth Avenue, New York, NY 10110

For information about special discounts for bulk purchases, please contact
W. W. Norton Special Sales at specialsales@wwnorton.com or 800-233-4830

Manufacturing by Toppan Leefung
Book design by Nick Caruso Design
Production manager: Devon Zahn

Library of Congress Cataloging-in-Publication Data

Names: Jones, Steve (Cheesemonger), author. | Lindsley, Adam, author.
Title: Cheese, beer, wine, cider : a field guide to 75 perfect pairings /
    Steve Jones & Adam Lindsley.
Description: New York, NY : The Countryman Press, a division of W. W. Norton
    & Company, [2019] | Includes bibliographical references and index.
Identifiers: LCCN 2018049014 | ISBN 9781682682432 (pbk.)
Subjects: LCSH: Food and wine pairing. | Food and beer pairing. | Cheese.
Classification: LCC TX911.3.M45 J66 2019 | DDC 641.01/3—dc23
LC record available at https://lccn.loc.gov/2018049014

The Countryman Press
www.countrymanpress.com

A division of W. W. Norton & Company, Inc.
500 Fifth Avenue, New York, NY 10110
www.wwnorton.com

978-1-68268-243-2 (pbk.)

10 9 8 7 6 5 4 3 2 1